# EFFECTIVE COMMUNICATION
# SKILLS

- ❖ Establish immediate rapport with others
- ❖ Initiate change
- ❖ Facilitate change
- ❖ Reduce stress
- ❖ Rebuild trust

- ❖ Diagnose and resolve internal conflict
- ❖ Deal with conflict effectively and efficiently
- ❖ Clarify difficult situations
- ❖ Develop a collaboration model
- ❖ Reduce misunderstandings and miscommunications!

## THE FOUNDATIONS FOR CHANGE

## JOHN NIELSEN

Copyright © 2008 by John Nielsen.

Library of Congress Control Number:     2007909203
ISBN:            Hardcover              978-1-4363-0468-9
                 Softcover              978-1-4363-0467-2

All rights reserved. No part of this book may be reproduced or transmitted in any form
or by any means, electronic or mechanical, including photocopying, recording, or by
any information storage and retrieval system, without permission in writing from the
copyright owner.

This book was printed in the United States of America.

**To order additional copies of this book, contact:**
Xlibris Corporation
1-888-795-4274
www.Xlibris.com
Orders@Xlibris.com
42556

# CONTENTS

## Effective Communication Skills

### Chapter 1
### Background Understanding

# Putting It All Together
## The Effective Communication Skills Workshop

### Chapter 2
### Workshop Introduction

### Chapter 3
### Communication Attitudes and Behaviors

## Chapter 4
### Addiction to Experience

## Chapter 5
### Self-awareness Skills: Thoughts, Feelings, and Self-talk

## Chapter 6
### The Language of Self-responsibility ("I" Statements)

## Chapter 7
### Self-awareness Skills: Responsibility for Interaction (Listening)

## Chapter 8
### Awareness Skills: Responsibility for Interaction (Feedback)

## Appendixes

# Acknowledgements

I want to acknowledge and thank all the people I've worked with over the past twenty years at Community of Grace. Their participation in doing small groups for the past twenty years has allowed us to use and refine the art of communication. We have worked with thousands of people in a variety of groups. Many of these same people have gone on to become facilitators, mediators, and team builders in their own sphere of influence. I'd like to thank my wife, Debbie, for her insight and support these past fifteen years. She has been a constant source of strength for me. The most important relationship has been my relationship with God. God has rewired my body, soul, and spirit to be able to understand why the truth sets me free.

# Preface

The idea of writing this book has evolved over the past twenty years from a strong desire to share with others the enormous gains that thousands of people have derived from their involvement with our recovery support group programs. Learning to communicate assertively has had a dramatic impact on the participant's lives including my own. Right from the beginning of our first assertiveness training in (1991), I became aware of how enormously valuable this material could be in helping others. In that time, I noticed the relationship between extremely low self-esteem and communication skills.

I think that this book is significantly enhanced by the combination of skills from our different types of professional training (*www.communication-empowerment.com*). My experience over the past twenty years has shown me how powerful this material is, and in writing this book, we are hoping to share some of our skills and insights.

This book offers an opportunity to people from all backgrounds to develop an improved understanding of assertiveness and to have at hand a basic training workbook from which they can apply these principles both to themselves and to others.

My aims for producing this book are the following:

- To demonstrate assertiveness as a valid communication skill relevant to trainer and trainee alike
- To encourage the use of assertiveness training within all organizations
- To demonstrate that the principles of assertiveness training are applicable to a wide variety of groups
- To provide a practical program that can be adapted for use at any level
- To provide a program for future use in teleseminars and Web simulcasts

# Introduction

# How to Use This Workbook

## How This Workbook Is Organized

This workbook comes in eight chapters. Each chapter covers its own topic though one chapter builds on previous ones. Before attending the Assertive Communication Skill Workshop, it is important that you read from here (page 13) through the feedback chapter ending on page 157. The rest of the workbook provides additional (optional) helps, information, and a list of other resources. Do be sure, however, to use the Feeling Word List on page 171 of the workbook. You may find it helpful to refer frequently to this resource.

Background Understanding (page 19)

The "Background Understanding" portion of this workbook, starting on page 19, explains what goes on in people as they interact with life, themselves, and other people. This understanding forms the foundation for effective communication skills.

Just as a person never stops eating, sleeping, exercising, and learning, there is always room for more personal growth. We never "arrive" though we can come to being able to live life peacefully and productively, both giving and receiving. Certainly one of the fundamental life skills is being able to communicate in ways that not only speak truth but draw people closer together in security and love; teaching those skills is the purpose of this course.

How can you become an assertive communicator?

1. Study this communication skills workbook.
2. Apply the principles until they become a part of you.
3. Repetition and practice is the key to development.
4. Develop good, strong self-management habits that allow you to monitor your practicing of the skills.
5. Use all the worksheets provided to help your practicing efforts.
6. Take advantage of the many advanced communication courses we offer at *www.communication-empowerment.com*

## Different Venues For This Course

This course can be used in a variety of venues. It can be used as a self improvement course or be used in conjunction with a teleseminar or webinare, as some people term it. It can also be used in small groups such as a recovery support group or a teambuilding group. The course materials and content are designed to be flexible and will work in any venue you choose.

Follow this plan, and you'll improve the way you communicate dramatically with others.

The Course Itself

The material that will be covered in the course itself starts on page 49 and goes through page 157.

More Information: The Self, Communication, and Recovery

Optional additional reading starts on page 159 and continues through the end of the workbook. These sections give more direction about using assertive communication as well as other recovery and emotional-healing suggestions and resources.

## How to Prepare for a Workshop

The following must be completed before attending the workshop:

- ☐ Complete all surveys accompanying the workshop and turn them in at least one week ahead of time, according to the workshop sponsor's instructions. By doing so, the results will be ready for you at the time of the workshop.
- ☐ READ the workbook through page 158. The appendix starts on page 159.
- ☐ Complete the charting exercises and worksheets scattered throughout the workbook. (The "Personal Commitment to Workshop Participation" on page 58 is the only page we ask you to share with the group. Any other answers you write on the worksheets in this workbook will remain confidential. At the workshop, you will have the opportunity to share as much or as little about them as you wish.)

## Using This Book with a Small Group

Go through the workbook together with friends. If you're going to be apart of an ongoing group or teleseminar, you'll want each group member to sign the Support Group Commitment on page 167. You must have an emotionally safe environment to practice in. And do realize that communication, as well as other people skills, are "more caught than taught." In other words, allow yourself to make mistakes, and remember that practicing the skills is the key.

## Beyond Effective Communication Skills

Consider attending our Advanced Team Building / Facilitator Training Workshop. This training moves the skill levels beyond the individual level to that of interacting with and leading groups. These team building and group dynamic skills apply to workplaces, homes, and any other places where people are trying to live and work together with shared goals and resources. For more information and workshop dates, see our Web site at *www.communication-empowerment.com*.

# Effective Communication Skills

# Chapter 1

# Background
# Understanding

# How Can Effective Communication Skills Help Me?

In a conversational situation, there are actually eight kinds of communication going on all at once:

- What I mean to say
- What I actually say
- What the other person hears
- What the other person thought they heard
- What the other person means to say
- What the other person actually says
- What I hear the person say
- What I think I heard the other person say

It's no wonder communication can be so confusing!

How can I take control of my life in such a way that things don't "drive me crazy." I may not be able to change all the circumstances (or the people!). But with effective communication skills, I can do the following:

- ✓ Be in control of myself
- ✓ Stop "them" from controlling me
- ✓ Make positive changes
- ✓ Strongly influence other people and my circumstances
- ✓ Find behaviors that help me feel safe, happy, and purposeful

## Life Benefits

Having a relationship with other people is one of the most important and wonderful things in this life and also one of the most difficult. If I don't know how to communicate in ways that really work, it is like trying to talk with someone who speaks a different language. We may both be good people, but a deep friendship just isn't going to happen, and what about the people that you do understand all too well. They may seem to be always giving you advice and not giving you any space to be yourself. Assertive communication can help you establish your right to have your own opinion, space, and life in a way that is respectful to yourself and to the other person. You may even find out that they really *do* or don't care about you and just didn't know how to show it!

## How Does God Expect Us to Talk?

*May the words of my mouth and the meditation of my heart be pleasing in your sight, O LORD, my Rock and my Redeemer.*
*(Psalm 19:14)*

*A man of knowledge uses words with restraint, and a man of understanding is even-tempered.*
*(Proverbs 17:27)*

*Reckless words pierce like a sword, but the tongue of the wise brings healing.*
*(Proverbs 12:18)*

*Why do you look at the speck of sawdust in your brother's eye and pay no attention to the plank in your own eye?*
*(Matthew 7:3)*

*A gossip betrays a confidence; so avoid a man who talks too much.*
*(Proverbs 20:19)*

*My dear brothers, take note of this: Everyone should be quick to listen, slow to speak and slow to become angry.*
*(James 1:19)*

> *He who answers before listening—that is his folly and his shame.*
> *(Proverbs 18:13)*
>
> *In your anger do not sin. Do not let the sun go down while you are still angry.*
> *(Ephesians 4:26)*
>
> *A patient man has great understanding, but a quick-tempered man displays folly. (Proverbs 14:29)*
>
> *The end of a matter is better than its beginning, and patience is better than pride. Do not be quickly provoked in your spirit, for anger resides in the lap of fools. (Ecclesiastes 7:8-9)*
>
> *Therefore encourage one another and build each other up, just as in fact you are doing. (1 Thessalonians 5:11)*

## What about Emotions? When . . . I Feel

There are ways to be the one who chooses how you feel. You don't have to let "them" ruin your day.

Look at the chart below in figure 1. It lists some common, irritating circumstances and some ways that we typically feel afterward. Lines connect the circumstances with the feelings. In this example, locking the keys in the car is followed by feeling angry, that I can't do anything right, and being out of control.

| | | |
|---|---|---|
| **W H E N** | I lock my keys in the car | angry |
| | my child gets in trouble at school | hurt |
| | my spouse comes home late | rejected |
| | my friend forgets our lunch date | that I'm a loser |
| | I am late for work | unloved |
| | my spouse keeps reading while I am talking | that I can't do anything right |
| | my boss frowns when I tell my idea | doomed |
| | my parents don't understand me | overwhelmed |
| | my computer crashes | crazy |
| | my family tracks mud across the clean carpet | out of control |

Figure 1. *When I lock my keys in the car,* I feel angry. I think that I can't do anything right, and I'm out of control. My emotion is anger.

# What Do You Want to Change in Your Life?

Your Own When . . . I Feel Chart

Figure 2 below is a blank chart for you to use. Pick several circumstances that sound like your life. Draw your own lines to describe your typical reactions to these circumstances. Go ahead and make lots of lines. Write in other "I feel" answers if you like.

| | | | |
|---|---|---|---|
| | I lock my keys in the car | | angry |
| | my child gets in trouble at school | I | hurt |
| W | my spouse comes home late | | rejected |
| H | my friend forgets our lunch date | F | that I'm a loser |
| E | I am late for work | | unloved |
| N | my spouse keeps reading while I am talking | E | that I can't do anything right |
| | my boss frowns when I tell my idea | E | doomed |
| | my parents don't understand me | | overwhelmed |
| | my computer crashes | L | crazy |
| | my family tracks mud across the clean carpet | | out of control |

Figure 2. Blank When . . . I Feel chart

## Your Top Priorities for Change

Now think about other negative circumstances that often happen to you. How do you feel when they happen? Which circumstances do you feel the worst about? Which ones are you most motivated to work on changing?

Choose the three circumstances that you would like to change. Write them on the lines below. Then add how you feel when they are happening. (You will be free to choose if you want to share any of this at the workshop or not.)

| When | I feel |
|---|---|
| When | I feel |
| When | I feel |

Figure 3. Top priorities for change

# Identifying Emotions and Thoughts

## Why Emotions?

Emotions can be hard to deal with. For some people, emotions are overwhelming. It seems that the emotions just take over and even define who they are. It is pretty scary to wonder when the next wave of strong emotions will come "out of nowhere" to wash over and drown you.

Yet other people say, "What emotions? What's all this fuss? Just do what you need to do and move on!"

It doesn't have to be that way. Hard to believe, but emotions can make us feel more alive, help us make better decisions, energize our actions, and still just be one part of us, not our whole identity. Emotions are supposed to be a tool that we use, but often it feels as though we are the tool, and the emotions are controlling us!

Babies are supposed to learn from their parents how to live with and understand emotions. How to have strong joy or excitement or strong anger yet still be themselves and have control. They are supposed to learn how to have strong emotions for a while and then return to peace (homeostasis). Those of us that never learned to regulate our emotions (to have *us* in control, not the feelings!) can still learn. Being in close relationship with safe people is how we learn to handle feelings.

The first step in learning to handle emotions is to identify what emotions I have and how to find the feelings that are results of thoughts (self-talk) such as "I'm a loser," "I can't do anything," or "No one likes me there."

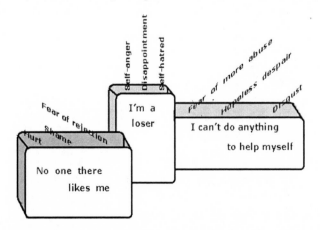

## Feelings Exercises

## Rewriting the When . . . I Feel Chart

Look again at the When . . . I Feel chart (figure 1 on page 23). Some of these "I feel" statements represent true feelings. Others are the beliefs (self-talk) that can accompany feelings.

Instructions
1. Which of the "feelings" listed below are feelings and which are thoughts (self-talk)? Answer "feeling" or "self-talk" in the Feeling or Self-talk? column.
2. For the rows that you said were actually self-talk, in the third column, write in what the underlying feelings might be.
3. *Unloved* and *overwhelmed* in column one have been done for you.

Hint: use the Feelings Word List on page 171 of this workbook.

| "I feel...." | Feeling or Self-talk ? | Underlying Feelings |
|---|---|---|
| angry | | |
| hurt | | |
| rejected | | |
| that I'm a loser | | |
| **unloved** | *Self-talk* | *rejected, hurt, depressed, disappointed* |
| that I can't do anything right | | |
| doomed | | |
| **overwhelmed** | *Feeling* | --- ---- --- |
| crazy | | |
| out of control | | |

Figure 4. Rewriting the When . . . I Feel chart

Some possible answers are shown on page 169.

# Look again at your "I feel" list.

Go back to the When . . . I Feel top priorities for change list you filled in on page 24 (figure 3). Analyze your "I feel" statements in the same way that we looked at the "I feel" statements in the previous exercise. Are your "feelings" really feelings, or are they thoughts or beliefs about yourself, other people, or maybe life in general? (We call the thoughts and beliefs that go on inside the head "self-talk.")

Instructions    1.    Turn to your When . . . I Feel top priorities for change list on page 24 (figure 3).

    2.    Copy the three "I feel" statements from page 24 into the "I feel" column in the chart below.

| "I feel...." | Feeling or Self-talk ? | Under-lying Feelings |
|---|---|---|
| | | |
| | | |
| | | |

Figure 5. Identifying true feelings in my top priorities for change list

    3.    Analyze each of the three "I feel" statements that you just copied above. If it represents true feelings, just write "feelings" in the Feelings or Self-talk? column.

    4.    If the "I feel" statement is actually a thought or belief, write "self-talk" in the Feelings or Self-talk? column.

    5.    For any "I feel" statements that turned out to be self-talk, make your best guess as to what your real feelings are. Write these feelings in the Underlying Feelings column.

    6.    For ideas, use the Feeling Word List on page 171 of this workbook.

# Self-talk

## What Is Self-talk?

Self-talk refers to the conversations that a person carries on mentally about self, about others, and about the environment. A person's self-talk can be consistent or inconsistent with what other people have actually said. Sometimes a person receives praise ("good job!") and turns it into criticism. (But he didn't notice where I really screwed up the job. If he saw that, then he wouldn't have said that I did such a good job. He would think I am as sloppy as the rest of the crew.) There can be a big difference between what was said and the individual's self-talk about it. How a person feels in a situation depends largely on what label he or she has assigned to it. Restructuring one's self-talk can change a person's overall experience of a situation, as well as initiate the process of behavior change.

Every person is like a large corporation, housed in the building of a body (brain). The conscious mind is like the President, sitting on the top floor with his/her feet on the desk while the Secretary, Research Clerk, and other parts of the nonconscious mind race around, taking care of business. The eyes, ears, and other senses are like the surveillance cameras all around the inside and outside of the building, continually monitored by another part of our brain that act as a Security Guard.

It is important to realize that the only part of our brain's functioning that we are consciously aware of is the "President." Most of our brain's receiving, analyzing, and deciding what to do happens in the nonconscious parts of the brain, and only a bit later do a few of the conclusions come to the attention of our conscious mind. We can look at what we are conscious of, though, to get clues as to what is going on in the nonconscious background.

How does the nonconscious part of the brain work? Here is an example:

> One day, just as the person starts to tell his great new idea to his boss, the Security Guard notices that the person's boss is frowning. Ooh, frowns are important! The guard decides that the frown means that there is a problem and shoots a memo off to the President (the person's conscious mind). It reads:

"Boss will not like the idea. You are going to be so embarrassed. How could I be so stupid as to think I have a worthwhile idea?"

The person gets the message, stops sharing the idea, and starts apologizing for wasting the boss's time. (Which only goes to prove that the idea really was dumb, right?)

The rapid-fire memos that the Security Guard sends to the conscious mind, or the President, are what we call self-talk. These messages tell us what we really believe (on a gut level) about

- ourselves;
- how safe other people are;
- what is good, bad, or scary;
- and what things mean.

We will talk more about self-talk and how you can change it in "The Brain" on page 38. For now, use the exercise below to practice identifying your own self-talk.

## Self-talk Samples

The chart below has some sample incidents (*when*), the resulting self-talk (*I tell myself*), and feelings (*and I feel*).

Notice that the And I Feel column includes the feeling messages from the physical body. We will talk more about reading feelings from our own and other people's bodies when we work on Observations (page 34).

Study the following samples, then complete your own chart on page 31.

| WHEN | I TELL MYSELF | AND I FEEL |
|---|---|---|
| When I receive an unexpected gift of $100 | I tell myself I don't deserve this. I should give it to someone who really needs it. | and I feel guilty, tight jaws, tense stomach |

| When | I tell myself | and I feel |
|---|---|---|
| Someone asks me to help them out | if I don't do what they ask, they won't like me | fragile, helpless, lost, over-whelmed, slumped shoulders |
| someone shares a problem | I need to fix it and tell them what to do | anxious, tight stomach |
| I share my frustration, and the other person interrupts and tells me what to do about it | My feelings don't count. I'm not smart enough to take care of myself. | shame, foolish, stupid, constricted gut, I want to leave |
| I need help from someone | If I ask and they say, "No," it means they don't like me. | fear of rejection, weak, insecure, shy, tight shoulders, rapid heart |
| someone close to me behaves in an embarrassing way | Why are they doing that? I need to make them stop | angry, agitated, critical, tight jaws, like I want to pace |

Figure 6. Self-talk samples (codependent behavior pattern)

# Identifying Self-talk in Your Top Priorities for Change

Let's clarify what you wrote in figure 3, top priorities for change, on page 24.

| | | |
|---|---|---|
| Expanding the top priorities for change | 1. | Copy the "when" scenarios from (figure 3) top priorities for change on page 24 into the figure below. |
| | 2. | From figure 5, identifying true feelings in my top priorities for change list on page 27, add your feelings to the And I Feel column. |
| | 3. | Imagine the "when" scenario, imagine the feelings, then listen inside to see what self-talk you have. The self-talk would be things like thoughts, beliefs, "I should" or "I/they always" statements, etc. Write the self-talk in the middle I Tell Myself column. |

| When | I tell myself | and I feel |
|------|---------------|------------|
| When | I tell myself | and I feel |
| When | I tell myself | and I feel |

Figure 7. Top priorities for change with self-talk

# A quick tip:

# Everybody Knows

When someone asks me to do something, should I say yes or no? I can read my body for a fast and accurate answer as to what I want.

- If my stomach tightens up and sinks, I really may not want to do it.
- If my stomach gets happy butterflies, I may want to say yes. Scan the rest of your body for clues. Self-talk is not always accurate for the event. Use self-talk as a clue-gathering exercise to discover what might be really going on. I will show you how to fix faulty self-talk as we get farther into the workbook. (Before saying yes, check the motivations. It can take practice to tell the difference between giving freely with no strings attached and dysfunctional giving.)

## Constructive Self-talk

Definition: Self-talk refers to the conversations, thoughts, and beliefs that a person carries on mentally about self, about others, and about the environment. A person's self-talk reflects his or her point of view and beliefs from experience.

Most self-talk is good. It helps me interpret what is happening, how to behave, and what may happen next. It allows me to respond quickly and smoothly to life without having to consciously analyze every circumstance, every detail.

- It lets me know to relax and expect happiness on my birthday. I noticed some friends' cars parked around the corner as I drove home, and now I hear noises in my "empty" house.

- On other days, it puts me on alert and tells me to be on guard when I arrive home and hear noises in the "empty" house.

## Destructive Self-talk

Some self-talk, however, "reflects thoughts and belief systems" that are harmful. These thoughts and beliefs keep me locked in belief and behavior patterns that hurt myself and others. This self-talk takes time and effort to change. With application of helpful self-talk, overtime positive change does occur.

Let's go back to the person trying to share a good idea with his boss when he notices the boss frowning ("What is Self-talk?" on page 28). Did you notice that the person never did find out for sure why the boss was frowning? But the brain takes the fact that he is *feeling some fear* as proof that there is something to be afraid of. And when he stops himself from sharing the idea with the boss, his brain takes it as further proof that his ideas are no good. *Do you want that kind of logic to control your life?*

We will learn in "Changing Self-talk" on page 43 of some simple ways to start taking control of the self-talk. And "Self-awareness Skills: Thoughts, Feelings, and Self-talk" on page 98 has even more about how to identify different types of harmful self-talk so we can make changes in our lives.

## Self-talk and Observation

### The Problem with Self-talk

Your brain is a marvelous creation. It can make sense out of very little information. Its habit of taking limited data and getting you an explanation quickly has probably saved your life several times.

For instance:

> While ambling across the street, from around the corner you hear
> a siren and squealing tires. You hurry off the road.

The brain is usually correct in its interpretation of small clues. So you forget that you didn't actually see a car speeding around the corner at you. It might have been a kid with a sound effects recording showing off to his friends. The only information you really have is the noise and its location.

## Definitions

Let's look at some definitions of what was going on and some possible perceptions:

Sensory data. The physical impressions themselves that the senses (sight, smell, touch, hearing, taste) receive:

- ✓ The sound of wailing and squealing
- ✓ The smell of hot asphalt
- ✓ The sunlight glaring off the buildings across the street
- ✓ The rumbling of a hungry stomach

Observation. What you notice about this sensory data:

- ✓ The sound of wailing and squealing was your only concern at this moment.

Self-talk. The rest of the story that the brain so busily provides:

- ✓ A high-speed police chase is coming my way! (perception)

Feelings. The emotional and bodily responses:

- ✓ Excitement, fear, rapid heartbeat

Behavior. The action you carry out:

- ✓ Run onto the sidewalk. Turn to see the noise source.

Wrong interpretations can really do a number on us physically and emotionally. Getting it right through the use of our communication skills model can change your life and health and relationships dramatically!

## Test Your Skill of Observation

Test time! What do you see here?

What do you see?

1. A man with a cold holding up a big Kleenex.
2. A snooping neighbor.
3. A Martian sneaking in your window to invade Earth.
4. Your neighbor, in a Martian costume, spying on you. Hide!
5. Other: _____

The brain is so often correct in its interpretation about what is going on around us that we usually just believe its conclusions. We just accept that what we *think* really is the *truth*. We don't stop and question ourselves. And we don't even notice the sensory data that the brain based its conclusions upon.

For instance, in the observation test above, what is it really?

    The correct answer is . . .

    ✓  A collection of lines and curves

Remember:

    This was an *observation* test,
    not a *self-talk* test ("the hungry Martians are coming!"),
    not a *feelings* test (danger! Fear of the future!),
    nor a *behavior* test (your neighbor hide!)

Most people were never taught to check out the accuracy of the self-talk their brain delivers. In my experience when it comes to interpersonal relationships, self-talk is wrong a lot more often than most people would guess.

## Becoming More Aware of Sensory Data

Observation (sensory data) Exercise

As you interact with people in the future, notice sensory data. Mindfully process the observations that you make.

Sensory data   • Body posture
to observe     • Tone of voice
               • Loudness of voice
               • Eye expressions
               • Mouth position
               • Facial complexion
               • Arm positions
               • Leg positions
               • Hand movements
               • Foot movements

Advanced practice: Before the workshop, practice your ability to observe. Notice your own voice and body clues.

## Avoid Misunderstandings

The "Feedback with a Guess" on page 152 will teach how to use observations to test the accuracy of your self-talk so you can avoid misinterpretations and get understanding and congruency in your communication with others.

# The Brain

## Your Brain: Taking Care of Business

Do you remember that "What is Self-talk?" on page 28 said that a person is like corporation with workers in the nonconscious part of the brain supplying feelings, information, predictions, and even decisions to the conscious mind, or the President?

Many separate parts of the brain work together, but not all of the parts are at work at the same the time. The *Security Guard*, of course, is *always* on duty, watching to see if anything important is going on. If something the person is seeing, sensing, thinking, or feeling is important, the Security Guard stamps the item as good, bad, or scary and sends it to the Research Clerk to see what else the person remembers about this. (If the item was bad or scary, the Security Guard may also send messages to the stomach to clamp down and to the heart to start racing.)

The *Research Clerk* retrieves other memories and information that seem related to this item. Then the other parts of the nonconscious brain, the Nonconscious Crew, come on duty to figure out what is probably going to happen and what the person should do about it. *Only after all this background preparation* does the President get notified about what is going on.

So it is that the conscious mind, the *President*, may suddenly become aware that his heart is pounding, palms are sweaty, and he really wants to leave NOW. He looks around, but all he notices is that a kitten unexpectedly walked into the room. He may never have heard the family story about when he was severely scratched by a cat at age two. That happened when he was too young to consciously remember the incident, but his nonconscious mind sure remembers. If the Nonconscious Crew does not get other training, it just stays on the alert, after all these years, trying to protect him from those "dangerous" cats. And the President will continue to find himself feeling and acting in ways that he does not like or understand.

Learning to consciously listen in on what messages the nonconscious mind is sending the conscious mind is an important first step in retraining that

Nonconscious Crew. We call this "identifying self-talk." Later, we will discuss ways to change the self-talk ("Changing Self-talk" on page 43).

## Wonderfully Made

The many skills of the Nonconscious Crew allow the President, our conscious mind, to not only see what is happening, but also have instant reports on previous times this has happened and what to expect next. The Nonconscious Crew even has a part that is always monitoring the face, voice, and body clues of the people around us and telling the President what the other people are feeling and probably thinking. This allows the President to make rapid, complex decisions in new situations. This is a good thing. The next section, however, talks about what happens if the Nonconscious Crew never receives the training it needs to do its job of supporting the President in the way it was designed to.

# The Brain

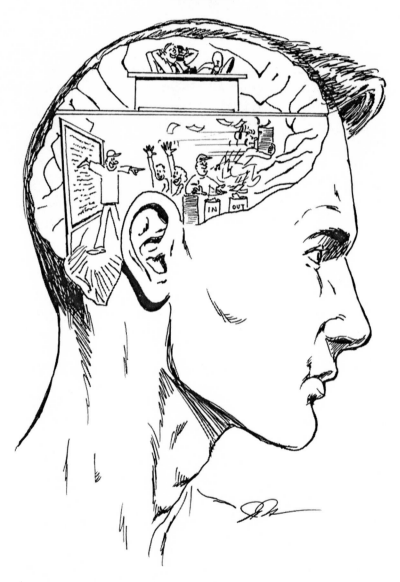

## Security Alerts

### Training the Nonconscious Crew

The brain originally learned from Mom (or primary caregiver) how to handle emotional situations. If Mom didn't know how to stay calm and act appropriately in hectic or scary situations, there is no way that the baby's brain can figure that out for itself. It is not a person's fault if they were never taught these emotional and behavioral skills. As adults, though, we are each responsible to do the work that it takes to learn whatever skills are missing. You have taken an important step in this direction by studying effective communication skills.

### "Danger, Danger, Something is Wrong!"

Sometimes, the "this is dangerous!" self-talk warnings from the security guard seem pretty silly. Why should we get so upset every time the house is a bit out of order? Think about how at times you get angry at others and the little messes they leave behind; you may feel as foolish as that arm-waving robot on *Lost in Space*. But you just can't stop yourself.

Through inner healing work, let's say I was to remember that my building contractor dad was always tidy . . . except when it rained, and he couldn't work. Then he would sit around the house watching TV, depressed and worrying about money. He would snarl at us and leave beer cans, food, and newspapers around the living room. Even Mom tried to avoid him, then. My Security Guard learned early on that *messy house* means *real danger*. The problem is no one has ever told my Nonconscious Crew that things are different now. My nonconscious mind still sees "mess" and yells, "Danger!"

### Code Red Alert, Batten All Hatches!

One job of the Nonconscious Crew is to coordinate a response when it gets the "Danger, Danger!" message from the Security Guard. However, only a very emotionally mature brain can calmly come up with good alternatives to handle stressful and difficult situations. Most of us never had anyone who even *knew* these emotional skills themselves, much less could teach them to our brains. So our nonconscious mind just doesn't have a clue about what to do during certain scary or stressful times.

The Security Guard is trying to protect its person from harm. But what can it do when it has a "Danger, Danger!" message with no good plan on how to handle it? If it sends the raw "Danger, Danger!" emotions to the President (our conscious mind), it will overwhelm and distort the logical, rational parts of our brain. So *it does the best it can*. It issues a red alert warning and *shuts down* the conscious, rational, logical higher brain parts. It takes them off-line. It does not allow the President to be in charge. Sometimes it doesn't even let the President know what is happening. Then it goes ahead and handles the situation in whatever way it always has.

## Triggers

No, we are not talking about the firing mechanism on a gun. For our purposes, a trigger is any event that causes the Security Guard to go into red alert mode.

In the messy house example earlier, the trigger was a messy house. The person may have been even-tempered but was messy. The fact is messy is just messy. Messy is not a fatal flaw in an otherwise kind person. But the Security Guard keeps insisting that messy also means selfish, snarly, dangerous, etc. So the wife snarled at the person about his mess before they had a chance to start snarling back. (Or at least, that is the Security Guard's logic. It is doing its best to keep the wife from being hurt.)

Remember how the Nonconscious Crew decides what is going on and what needs to be done before even telling the President anything (page 38)? Watch for when you are feeling happy or quiet, then suddenly are upset, tense, or angry. What happened? What was the trigger? What did the Nonconscious Crew think was so important or dangerous? Identifying our personal triggers and the self-talk they cause is a powerful step in retraining the Security Guard and the rest of the nonconscious mind.

## Retraining the Nonconscious Crew

The good news is the brain's Nonconscious Crew can be retrained. It can learn better ways to handle stressful and scary situations. It can learn to keep the President informed and in charge so the brain can make conscious, rational decisions about what to do even when life gets hard. (And it can learn that the wife's husband is not the same as her father.)

Learning assertive communications skills is one step in the retraining process. These skills help the brain identify the truth about itself, situations, and other people. Assertive communication will allow me to stop attacking other people and to start telling them that while I don't like their messes, I still value and cherish them as people.

The next section of this workbook has more about how to identify and change self-talk so that the Nonconscious Crew can be retrained.

## Changing Self-talk

Here are three ways to change your self-talk:

✓ Identify and redefine (talk back to self-talk)
✓ Get support
✓ Get new management

Read about these techniques below.

For more tips, see "Self-awareness Skills: Thoughts, Feelings, and Self-talk" on page 98 and "Making Changes" on page 43.

## Identify and Redefine (Talk back to self-talk)

Write out the damaging self-talk. Then write what is true.

Just because you have always believed something doesn't make it true! Writing out the self-talk and talking back to it with truth takes away a lot of the old self-talk's power. Here are some examples of talking back to self-talk:

| When | Old Self-talk | Truth |
|------|---------------|-------|
| I receive an unexpected gift of $100. | I don't deserve this. I should give it to someone who really needs it. | It's OK to have fun. I can share some of my things, but I am important too. |
| Someone asks me to help them out. | If I don't do what they ask, they won't like me. | Saying no is a way of taking care of myself. If someone cares about me, they will understand when I need to say no. |
| Someone shares a problem. | I need to fix it and tell them what to do. | I can't really fix anyone else's. I can listen for a short time to show I care, then go do something else. |
| When I share my frustration, the other person interrupts and tells me what to do about it. | My feelings don't count. I'm not smart enough to take care of myself. | This person is not really listening to me. My feelings are important. Maybe I should talk with someone else. |
| I need help from someone. | If I ask and they say no, it means they don't like me. | I can ask for help and help others when they need it. I may need to ask several people before I find the right help. |

"Self-awareness Skills: Thoughts, Feelings, and Self-talk" on page 98 has more details about identifying destructive self-talk.

Now practice changing your own self-talk:

Go back to page 31, figure 7, top priorities for change with self-talk. Copy the When and I Tell Myself (Self-talk) columns into the table below. Then write in what would be the truth about that situation. You may need to get help to figure this out from someone further along in recovery.

| When | I tell myself | but the truth is |
|------|---------------|------------------|
| When | I tell myself | but the truth is |
| When | I tell myself | but the truth is |

Figure 8. Top priorities for change, replacing self-talk with truth

## Support and Retraining

A brain's Nonconscious Crew learns new coping patterns by being in safe relationships with other people.

People's brains learn how to cope gracefully with stress and pain only from talking and sharing with other people. From safe relationships, we can receive the comfort of having our thoughts and feelings really "heard." And as we watch others model how they are coping with problems, our Nonconscious Crew can pick up new patterns, new states of mind.

Join a support group or one of our teleseminars. Being apart of these types of groups will give you a vehicle and a platform to practice and learn healthy communication skills and to share your thoughts and feelings. Make friends with people that seem to have healthy, positive attitudes and *spend time with them*. The quality of the people we share our lives with largely determines the eventual quality of our own lives. People that take risks to grow with you in these groups will enhance your growth and develop a positive model of community for your future.

*Keep learning* all you can through our telesemiars or your local support group environment and continue making time with positive people. Those old habits of isolating, of staying separate and saying, "I have to do everything myself," will keep trying to drag you away from being with people. The self-talk will say, "Why should I bother other people with my problems?" "What's wrong with me that I can't figure it out by myself?" and "If you need other people, you are just weak and setting yourself up to be hurt."

## I Got New Management

I was not made to live alone, not even on my insides. The god that made me never designed me to do life by myself. I was designed to live in cooperation with him, to always have him right alongside, helping me out.

I asked him to come and take over the management of my whole being. The Bible has a lot to say about how to heal that Nonconscious Crew and get your self-talk healthy and positive. Jesus Christ came to take all the pain, hurt, and damage that I had received and that I had given to others. Jesus took it all to himself when he died on the cross and offered to give me a healthy new life instead. Parts of that new life may come suddenly; other parts will take hard work to get the old self-talk to change enough to let the new life in. But God will never give up on you.

You don't believe in God? Or you are too angry at him to talk to him? That's OK. You can ask him to help with that too. Tell him what you feel and that you need him to show you the truth. He can handle up-front, honest communication! God is a safe one to practice some of those "When this happens, this is how I feel" statements on!

# Putting It All Together

# The Assertive Communication

# Skills Workshop

# Chapter 2

# Workshop Introduction

## Personal Commentary

Again, I want to reiterate some things. The Effective Communication Skills Workshop you are about to encounter has been an outcome of twenty years of my personal recovery journey plus the training on group dynamics I received from the University of Arizona in 1989. The university contracted with the Department of the Navy to conduct forty-hour group training and intervention workshops to increase awareness of drug and alcohol related issues. During that time, I worked for the university facilitating these groups. I was able to log in hundreds of hours of group processing time. In 1991, I started a recovery program at Community of Grace Church (Restoration Depot) called RAPHA (the Lord that heals). This program is now known as "Steps of Grace." Since that time, we have ministered to thousands of people and trained many facilitators in using proper group dynamic skills. These communication and facilitative skills have been foundational in the success of this program. The skills are basic but powerful if applied properly.

## Overview

As you proceed through this workshop, you will first learn how to talk more effectively about individual issues. Secondly, you will learn how to listen to others' issues. Next, the program combines these individual skills into interpersonal and group processes for interacting more collaboratively. You will learn by doing. Communication skills are caught, not taught.

> Learning the skills requires practice with a combination of group interaction, facilitator modeling, and interactive learning techniques.

Finally, the interpersonal styles wrap up a package I feel will prepare you for getting the most out of any small group and enhance your ability to improve your overall communication skills with other areas of your life.

Above all else, I want to give Jesus Christ all the glory because it was he who taught me to be truthful. First Corinthians 13 tells us that "love rejoices in the truth." God is love, so God rejoices in the truth. Jesus spoke about the truth in John 8:32. Jesus said to the Jews who believed in him, "If you continue to obey my teaching, you are truly My followers. Then you will *know* [emphasis mine] the truth and the truth will *make you free* [emphasis mine]." Truth and openness are prerequisites for your successful communication skills development journey.

Through this workshop, I'd like to impart and share with you that which the Lord has given me in the area of communication skills. As you then learn and apply these skills to your life, both individually and in the group process, God will use these tools to grow and equip you to come alongside others. This is walking out the truth that he gives us in 2 Corinthians 1:3-7.

## 2 Corinthians 1:3-7

## The Rescue

*All praise to the God and Father of our Master, Jesus the Messiah! Father of all mercy! God of all healing counsel! He comes alongside us when we go through hard times, and before you know it, He brings us alongside someone else who is going through hard times so that we can be there for that person just as God was there for us. We have plenty of hard times that come from following the Messiah, but no more so than the good times of His healing comfort—we get a full measure of that, too.*

*When we suffer for Jesus, it works out for your healing and salvation. If we are treated well, given a helping hand and encouraging word, that also works to your benefit, spurring you on, face forward, unflinching. Your hard times are also our hard times.*

> *When we see that you're just as willing to endure the hard times as to enjoy the good times, we know you're going to make it, no doubt about it.*
>
> —*The Message*

I pray that this workshop will be a growing experience for you. Enjoy this encounter with truth and freedom. Most importantly, allow God to open up your awareness of his healing and new growth opportunities.

## Introduction

### Goal

- To equip future participants with a set of communication strategies, skills, and processes for dialoguing and swapping information in a win-win situation rather than a win-lose situation

- To model safety in group interaction, as well as encouraging a deep level of sharing that is strived for in a healthy support group

### Objectives

#### Awareness

- To increase awareness of yourself, others, and your group

- To increase awareness of who is responsible for what and who has the power for what

- To learn to take purposeful action for improvement in the way you communicate with others

- To readjust your stress and belief systems

- To improve your motivation through self-empowerment

- To distinguish interpersonal styles of communication and the impact on self and others

Skills

- To learn talking and listening skills for sending and receiving clear, effective messages

- To learn talking and listening skills for creating understanding and building relationships by practicing the use of self-disclosure and strategic listening for gaining complete and clear information about yourself and others

- To build safety and confidence by encouraging others to look deeper and self-disclose

Processes

- To learn processes for taking personal responsibility for interaction with others

- To learn how to grow with yourself and the group through coaching and personal participation

- To participate in various groups interaction assignments

Choices

- To demonstrate openness when interacting with others that would include sharing your thoughts, feelings, and self-talk as well as listening attentively to others

- To apply the skills and processes using "here and now" situations

- To take personal responsibility for yourself by using "I" statements throughout the training

Benefits

- Get to the core issues faster with less stress and better understanding.

- Gain deeper levels of disclosure and meaning.

- Encourage ongoing disclosure.

- Reduce fear and defensiveness and increase trust with self and others.

- Relate more openly to others.

- Create a win-win atmosphere with yourself and others.

- Reveal areas of denial so healing can take place.

- Feel comfortable in sharing your unhealthy self-talk.

- Feel good about revealing truth within yourself even when it's uncomfortable.

- Improve your ability to give sensory data.

- Increase your options for gaining more in-depth understanding of others.

## Group Dynamics

Groups go through many stages before they become healthy and mature. In the initial stages, groups are asking themselves many questions:

Who are these people?
Will I be in or out of this group?
If I join, how involved will I be?
Do I belong here? Will they accept me?
Do these people like me? Do I like them?
How much do I want to risk?

Can I really trust these people?
What's this group really about?
What's expected of me?
Do I fit and belong in here?
Can I be myself and be a part of this group?
Can I say what I want without being judged?

A healthy support group has the freedom, with established ground rules, to dialogue with each other in the group process. It usually takes two to three meetings for a group to gel so to speak.

> A group starts growing in greater depth and vulnerability when they start talking and sharing with each other.

The trust level in a group increases as people trust. Coaching and modeling by the facilitator is paramount in the development of the group and is a barometer of safety as the group matures.

> Learning the fundamental communication skills builds a foundation for trust, self-awareness, and the modeling of effective communication skills.

## Caring, Sharing, and Communication

Every communication between two people contains two components: attitude and behavior. Attitudes derive from the combined beliefs, feelings, and intentions you hold. Behaviors, the verbal and nonverbal actions you take, reflect and stem from your underlying attitudes. So each exchange you make with others reflects our underlying attitude about yourself and others.

Behavior = observable words and actions

Attitude = underlying beliefs, feelings, and intentions

Two basic attitudes you can hold toward yourself are the following:

❖ I don't care about me (count, value, consider).

❖ I care about me (count, value, consider).

In every situation, you communicate either that you do not value, respect, and count yourself—you do not care—or that you do.

Likewise, two corresponding attitudes you can hold toward others are the following:

❖ I don't care about you (count, value, consider).

❖ I care about you (count, value, consider).

Again, in any exchange, you communicate either that you do not value, respect, and count others—you do not care—or that you do.

The choice is constantly ours. Which will we communicate? "I care" or "I don't care."[1]

Motivation, Self-empowerment, and Communication

Motivation is the quality of having a motive or incentive that stirs us to action toward our goals and objectives. The mind of a motivated person is filled with targets, objectives, and pictures of excellence. The motivated communicator is able to picture the destination. A motivated communicator knows where he wants to go and has the will and perseverance to get there.

Motivation propels us toward our objectives. Fear and stress hinders us from reaching our goals unless we respond with purposeful action. Learning and applying the effective communication skills in this workshop will increase

---

[1.] Parts of caring, sharing and communication are excerpted from *Couple Communication* I, by Sherod Miller (Interpersonal Communication Programs).

your self-empowerment to change negative learned behaviors and habits so you can get the most out of your communication with yourself and others.

## Group Guidelines

- Make yourself comfortable. Please wear comfortable clothing.

- Each group will generate their own ground rules at the beginning of the workshop.

- Expect to be coached by the facilitator. Feedback is essential for learning.

- Please come prepared to participate.

- Open up from your own life. (The group will often open up to each other only as much as the other group members open up to them.)

- Take the risk to use the new skills as you learn them.

- Allow yourself to make mistakes.

- Have fun.

- Please complete all preassigned workshop homework as listed on the next page.

## Workshop Preassigned Homework

Communication Style Testing (May not be available in your area)

We use profile testing to help you in determining your communication style attributes. Knowing how your communication style differs from those you live and work with will help you more accurately understand others and make yourself more understandable to them. Before the workshop, do the following:

- Carefully read the test instructions.

- Thoughtfully fill out the test result pages.

- RETURN THE COMPLETED TEST at least TWO WEEKS BEFORE THE WORKSHOP.

- You will receive your test results and an explanatory booklet at the workshop.

- During the workshop, I will give a brief overview of how your test results can affect understanding your personality, relationships, and success in team building. With increased self-awareness of self and others, you will better understand the communication process and develop better insight for group dynamics and the facilitative process.

---

Preassigned Workshop Homework

Read this workbook through page 157.

The final section of this workbook, the appendix, starting on page 159, is optional.

Complete the worksheets on the following pages before the workshop:

You will be asked to share with the group what you write on the first form:

- Personal Commitment to Workshop Participation, page 58

---

Sharing the remaining forms with the group is optional, but do complete them before the workshop:

- Susceptibility to Addiction, page 85
- Relationship Questionnaire, page 86
- Adaptability Patterns Questionnaire, page 88
- Stages of Dependency and Addiction Questionnaire, page 93
- Dependency Log, page 95
- Experience to Pressure page, 110

## Commitment

Just by being a part of this workshop says a lot about your commitment to learning new skills and increasing your self-awareness. By filling out the Personal Commitment to Workshop Participation form, you'll be thinking about how you're going to choose to participate in the workshop. Be sure to fill this form out before the workshop since you will be sharing this group commitment form with the person who interviews you and introduces you to the group.

### Personal Commitment to Workshop Participation

State how you plan to participate and contribute to this class

1. How I plan to participate and contribute to this workshop:

    a. What I will do is _____
    _____

    b. When I will do it is _____
    _____

    c. What I will need is _____
    _____

2. Reaching my goal:

   a. What might I say to myself that would stop me from achieving my goal?

      _____

      _____

   b. What will I do to ensure that I reach my goal?

      _____

      _____

3. The person in this workshop that I choose to observe my participation is:

   _____

   _____

4. This person will assist me this week in the following ways:

   a. What I'd like this person to do is _____

      _____

   b. What I'd like this person to say is _____

      _____

5. I will evaluate my results in the following ways at the following times:

   _____

   _____

_____          _____
Signature (self)                Signature (observer)

_____
Date

## Building Rapport Group Exercise

Complete this form *at the workshop* with a partner:

The goal of this exercise is to help us all get acquainted with each other. The group will be divided into pairs. Each person will take a turn interviewing the other person. Use this form to fill in information about your partner.

During the interview, you will also share and sign the Personal Commitment to Workshop Participation on the previous page.

We will then reconvene, and each person will introduce to the group the person they interviewed.

1. The name of the person I am introducing: _____
   _____
   _____


2. What types of physical activities does s/he enjoy?
   _____
   _____
   _____


3. What does s/he do for relaxation?
   _____
   _____
   _____


4. What is difficult in his/her life?
   _____
   _____
   _____


5. One thing that is important in his/her life is
   _____
   _____
   _____

6.  Three things s/he likes about his/her self are

_____

_____

_____

7.  One thing s/he wants to walk away with from this workshop is

_____

_____

_____

# Chapter 3

# Communication Attitudes and Behaviors

*He that hath knowledge spareth his words; and a man of understanding
is of an excellent spirit.*

*—Proverbs 17:27*

*He who restrains his words has knowledge, and he who is calm of spirit
is a man of understanding.*

*—Berkeley*

---

Goal

- To let those participants distinguish among the types of behavioral responses to situations and to examine the value of assertiveness in their relationships and make the changes necessary to insure that they are able to develop a support network for assistance in goal achievement.

- To examine your interpersonal styles and explore the risk, the trade-offs, and consequences of the choices of your individual style

Objectives

- To specify the behaviors associated with aggressive, passive-aggressive, passive and assertive response

- To identify your use of the different interpersonal choices during the workshop and in different situations

---

- To explore the consequences of the various interpersonal styles you use

- That participants will recognize how the principles of economy and control apply to behavior

- That participants will practice assertiveness skills in various role-playing exercises involving situations where they typically behave passively or aggressively

For many people, a lot of their stress comes from trying to talk to and get along with other people. One way to cut out some of this stress is by learning to speak honestly and directly, in other words, by using effective communication skills.

Say What You Mean
and Ask for What You Want!

## Lack of Assertiveness

Effective communication literally dies because people would rather die, it seems, than to express themselves assertively. "Communication" comes from a Latin word that means "to make common." The word "assertiveness" also comes from a Latin word that means "to join to oneself." Put the two together, and what you are doing is "making common (known) what belongs to you." For example, "You're standing on my foot!"

If you take these origins into account, assertiveness has gotten a bad rap. Being assertive is a basic survival tool for human relations and certainly for protecting every priority list. To be assertive means you adhere to the following practice:

I say what I mean and ask for what I want!

Assertiveness is not and should not be confused with the two extremes: aggressiveness and passivity.

Assertiveness is not *aggressiveness*, which is often when you end up saying something you regret. Aggressiveness shows no consideration for the other person. An aggressive person walks in and totally takes over a situation, mashing beneath himself anything that dares get in his way. It's knowing you're standing on someone else's foot and not moving!

Assertiveness is also not *passivity*. Passive people never finish their priority lists because they are always changing the lists or adding to them (codependency). But because passive people never speak up, there is the silent acceptance or approval of the new project no matter how trivial or unrelated to the project or situation that it might be. It's allowing someone to continue to stand on your foot. The passive person never speaks up. Instead, the emotion and energy (and pain?) are all kept inside. People who do this long enough end up killing themselves by the stress and pressure they create within. They are also not being honest with the people around them. (Incidentally, the Latin origin of this word is *passivius*—capable of suffering.)

What is assertiveness? Assertiveness is saying, "I have a problem (and you are the problem?)" This is what's happening. This is what it's doing to me. And this is what needs to be done. This is what I want.

With practice, you can become great at assertiveness; so please, don't throw assertiveness out the window just because it doesn't work for you every single time. Assertive thinking and an assertive response will always be better for your own mental health and well-being and, at the same time, will make you a more honest person. Remember—assertiveness is not aggressiveness—assertive statements can be made in a direct but nonconfrontational ways (the workshop will show you how).

Assertive communication requires thinking and practice, but eventually, it can become a natural part of one's everyday behavior. Assertive communication will not solve all problems. People are entitled to make their own choice about how they will react. In fact, telling the truth, even when spoken tactfully and appropriately, may shake up some relationships. However, using assertive communication will help a person feel calm and in control while relating with other people.

## Communication Styles

Not every conversation needs careful communication skills. Sometimes people just need to ask some fact questions like the following:

- What time is Susie's dentist appointment?

- Does the dog get one cup of food or two?

- What's the next step on this project?

Or they want to chitchat. That is fine.

But when it is important that the message is received properly, even good relationships can be sabotaged by communicating the right information in a destructive way.

Some questions that you can ask yourself are the following:

- What is my usual mode of behaving?

- What are the consequences of that particular mode?

- What are the trade-offs and/or risks involved in the different interpersonal choices I make?

- Which one of these behaviors could be more productive in my communications with others?

Read these definitions of four communication styles and then the examples that follow:

| Aggressive | Passive (Nonassertive) | Passive-aggressive (Indirect Aggression) | Assertive |
|---|---|---|---|
| Taking care of my rights and disregarding the rights of others. | Taking care of others' rights with manipulation. | Taking care of others' rights at my expense. | Taking care of my rights and respecting others' rights. |
| I get what I want at your expense. | You get what you want, but you'll pay a price for it. | I don't get what I want. | I sometimes get what I want. |

As you can see, assertive communication follows the principle of control and economy.

> Assertive communication means "saying what needs to be said."
> No more and no less.

It also increases the chances that a person's point of view will be heard and respected because it is stated in a way that does not violate others' rights. It is not necessarily the best response in every situation but rather it may be a more balanced way to interact in terms of trade-offs. Something to pay attention to is that there can be confusion between aggressive and assertive behavior. You have more than likely noticed that there are times that assertive interaction is described as aggressive interaction. That is an opportunity for you to look at the differences between the behaviors as noted in the above diagram and ask yourself questions that will help you clarify, "Is this aggressive or assertive behavior?" In other words, "Am I taking care of my rights at the cost of another's rights?" OR "Am I taking care of my rights AND respecting the other's rights?"

People are entitled to make their own choices as to how they will act in situations. However, certain choices that people make may influence their resulting thoughts, body responses, emotions, and future actions. In every interpersonal situation, people have the choice of acting in an assertive, aggressive, passive-aggressive, or nonassertive manner.

## Aggressive

Aggressive behavior. Aggressive behavior is acting in a manner that allows a person to try to get what he or she wants no matter what the cost to anyone else. A person who uses aggressive behavior may feel angry or frustrated. Aggressive behavior includes threatening, accusing, fighting, and attacking behavior.

The aggressive style is in-your-face and often leaves the hearer feeling defensive, ashamed, or hurt. It may clearly communicate the same information as the assertive style, but it is usually a "you are the problem" statement that leaves it hard for the hearer to feel safe responding at all. You do know where the aggressive communicator stands, but this style certainly does not extend an invitation for more personal disclosure and dialogue!

## Aggressive Examples

- The next time you borrow my car and do a stupid thing like leaving me with an empty gas tank, our friendship is over.

- Finish this task, or you're fired.

- If you can't see what I'm talking about, you're stupid.

- I don't care what it costs you in time, just get it done.

- Your time is not important to me. Just do as I say.

- You are incompetent and lazy!

## Passive

Passive behavior. Passive behavior is acting in a manner that allows other people to get what they want at the expense of oneself. Sometimes a person who uses passive behavior may feel helpless or out of control. Passive behavior includes waiting, receiving, and enduring without resistance to what others impose. Sometimes a person who acts passively becomes angry and then acts aggressively in an effort to regain control.

The passive communicator seems like such a nice person who gets along with everyone and never causes arguments. A passive-style person may have been taught that asking for what one wants is being selfish. Or it may not have been safe, growing up, to express individuality. Whatever the cause, a passive-style person takes all the blame and responsibility but doesn't seem to have his own opinions, wants, and preferences. Often, the negative feelings, which don't get expressed outwardly, end up eating away at the person's own physical health. There is also a good chance that the passive person will explode inappropriately because they cannot hide their anger any longer.

Because the passive style does not state what the wants and feelings are, it leaves the hearer guessing as to the feelings or even what the facts are! The hearer often leaves the conversation feeling ashamed or guilty but can't quite figure out why.

## Passive Examples

- It's OK that you just told a lie to other people about me. I'll get over it. *(I actually want to punch him in the face.)*

- The boss just sexually harassed me. I'll just endure it. Maybe he will stop.

- My supervisor always swears at me. It's just part of the job.

- He told me to wait a few minutes. It's now been an hour. I don't want to hurt his feelings by leaving.

## Passive-aggressive

Passive-aggressive behavior. Passive-aggressive behavior is acting in a manner that allows a person to try to get what he or she wants by indirect, subtle means. A person who uses passive-aggressive behavior may feel angry, but he or she also may feel helpless. Passive-aggressive behavior is an indirect effort to control others and is sometimes difficult to interpret. Passive-aggressive behavior includes sarcasm or unkind words, procrastination and dawdling, and/or inefficiency or forgetfulness. All of these behaviors are indirect expressions of hostility, indirect ways of resisting authority, or indirect means of controlling others. Passive-aggressive behavior is more common than either passive behavior or aggressive behavior. It is sometimes very subtle and appears more socially acceptable than aggressive behavior.

The passive-aggressive communication style, like the passive, never quite states what the speaker is feeling or wanting. But the communication does include some aggressive zingers that leave the hearer feeling wounded though he might not be able to pin down just what the speaker said that hurt so much. We often refer to this style as the "backdoor approach."

## Passive-aggressive Examples

- I'll just drag my feet on the job. That will certainly irritate them.

- *(I would like the window opened.)* Hey, is that window nailed down or something?

- *(I'm in a restaurant and my order hasn't arrived on time.)* Hey, are you still killing the cow?

- *(Bad service.)* Hey, who's the customer, me or you?

- Dear, what do you think I am, stupid?

- *(At an ugly mess.)* Well, that certainly looks appealing!

## Assertive

Assertive behavior. Assertive behavior is acting in a manner that allows a person to try to get what he or she wants but does not violate the rights of others. An assertive person often gives people feedback about how their behavior is affecting him or her. For example, "When you cut in line in front of me, I get very angry." Assertive behavior can also mean planning a course of action and sticking to it. An example of this could be, "I'm wondering if there's a way for both of us to succeed here?" Assertive behavior is a skill that a person can use, but the use of the skill will not always produce what the person wants.

The assertive communication techniques taught in this course enable the speaker to say what is important while minimizing the chance that the hearer will react defensively, feel attacked, or feel the need to attack back. Of course, the hearer still may react badly no matter what you do. But when you explain your feelings about it, even telling another person what you don't like about their actions is easier for them to take. Other communication styles, though, almost guarantee hurt feelings and destructive reactions.

## Assertive Examples

- When you borrow my car, then return it with the gas almost empty, I usually discover it while I am hurrying to an appointment. I feel frightened that I will run out of gas. When you use the car, if you bring it back even just half full, that works for me.

- I seems to me that you're always fifteen minutes late. When you do that, I'm telling myself that you don't care about how that might be affecting me. When you do that, I label your behavior as disrespectful, and I'm finding myself resenting you. What are you willing to do to change that behavior?

- When you continue to do what you say you are not going to do, I get really confused. I'm telling myself that you really don't want to change. It would be easier for me if you'd just say yes or no and stick to it. What do you think?

- When I see you drag your feet and take your time on a regular basis, I'm telling myself that you don't like what you are doing. Is there something that you are unhappy with that is causing this behavior?

## Short and to the Point

Notice that the assertive communication style gets directly to the point. It does not confuse or hide the issue by beating around the bush or being apologetic. It "says what needs to be said" and is done.

## It's OK to Be Assertive

If we are accustomed to a more passive communication style, then even appropriate assertive communication statements can feel aggressive. A quiet, "I would rather not have fried sea slug again tonight, thanks," can feel rude; and the self-talk may say, "Ooh, if you say that, he will be so offended. He'll think you don't even care about him!" So before believing the feelings (that what you were about to say is just too rude and aggressive), think about it:

| Is what I want to say | • About me and not blaming someone else? |
|---|---|
| | • Am I stating facts (observations) and not labeling? |
| | • Am I telling what is true for me while not trying to make someone else change? |

If so, it is probably an appropriate communication. Go for it!

# Will the Real Me Please Stand Up?

## Our Many Selves

Remember that many of the specialized parts of the brain only function when they are needed ("Your Brain: Taking Care of Business" on page 38). As we face a situation, the nonconscious mind decides which parts of the brain will be needed, then calls them to active duty. If we are taking a math test, let's hope that it tells the logical parts of the brain to get active, along with quiet concentration and tuning out distractions. If we are relaxing with friends, it may decide that parts of the brain that can make up silly jokes and have fast reflexes (that will duck at flying water balloons) will work better. Believe me, turning off silly jokes during a math test is a GOOD IDEA.

Overtime, some of the same groups of brain parts keep getting called to active duty at the same time. If logic, concentration, and no distractions work together often in math class, they develop into the brain's math team. A group of brain parts that gets accustomed to working together as a practiced team is called a *state of mind*. The brain can quickly call up the brain team it needs by switching to another state of mind. Want to observe brains instantly change their state of mind? Just watch ten-year-old boys' behavior the moment they leave school and are alone with friends! Instant brain switch-a-roo!

*States of mind* that get used a lot become one of our *selves*. Every person is made up of many selves, each with its own specialty, available to be active at a moment's notice. You don't have to constantly figure out everything from scratch, just dial up the self that knows what to do! Some selves we may have are

✓ a math-student self,
✓ a silly-with-good-friends self,
✓ an on-the-job self,
✓ an I'm-being-physically-attacked self that drops into a karate stance,

✓ a with-family self
✓ a child self when visiting parents at the family home,
✓ a parent self for our own kids,
✓ a church self, and
✓ an I'm-relaxing-just-let-me-veg self.

## I Have to Be Me!

I may have the idea that my real self is fearful or angry or maybe "a loser." I am sure that this is the real me. It is "just the way I am," and "a tiger can't change his stripes."

Babies are born with their own personality traits, like being generous, being musically inclined, being detail-oriented, having mechanical skills, etc. These types of traits are part of who a person really is. It is important for a person to discover the treasures that are inside that make up the real me.

But identities like fearful, angry, or loser are not some of the hidden treasures that make up the real me. They are just a self (a set of brain responses) that has built up over years of practice until it seems like the very definition of who I am. And when I hear the idea that I don't have to be fearful, angry, or a loser, a part of me screams, "You are killing ME!"

When I choose to

- act assertively instead of fearfully,

- communicate about a problem before the anger builds up,

- and risk trying again even if I didn't succeed last time,

it will feel like I am "just pretending" or "am a fake." But what is "fake" is the fearful, angry, or loser idea. By acting differently, I am actually starting to be more truthful!

## Finding the Real Me

Finding out who I really am takes being close to safe, loving people that can tell me what they see in me (give me feedback). Their feedback helps me sort out who I really am and supports me as I grow into living as the real me.

# Making Changes

Here are additional techniques and information that can help you start changing self-talk and living more peacefully. These continue the list started in "Changing Self-talk" on page 43 and continued in "Self-awareness Skills: Thoughts, Feelings, and Self-talk" on page 98.

These techniques are most successful when used with the regular encouragement and feedback of support groups and other friends that are on the same journey. Simply stated, healthy relationships are where it's at. But you already knew that, that is why you are taking this communication course!

## Choose to Change Behavior

Remember that the brain reads the body's signals as part of how it figures out what it is feeling and what is going on. Standing up straight, looking people in the eye, speaking with a clear firm voice, smiling, speaking up even when you feel shy, trying something even though you are frightened, all send signals not only to other people, but also to yourself!

For example, there are studies in which people rate items as to how good or bad they are. The people who are told to put a smile on their face tend to rate things as better than people who make their face frown while they are going over the same list. Apparently, the brain notices the smile and is nudged into a state of mind that thinks, "Things must be good because I am smiling." So it evaluates the things on the list as being better than it does when frowning.[1]

You won't feel like doing it at first. In fact, there will probably be some very loud self-talk that tells you the following:

- You are crazy.

- You are lying by acting how you don't really feel.

- Disaster is about to happen.

---

[1.] Daniel J. Siegel, *The Developing Mind: How Relationships and the Brain Interact to Shape Who We Are* (Guilford Press, 1999), 143.

How can anyone ever successfully change behavior patterns with all this ruckus coming from the Security Crew? Their arguments can feel very convincing!

The first time a person

   ✓  says no when he was feeling pressured to say yes or

   ✓  tells his feelings and is heard

   ✓  or does something that was scary.

The first surprise will be that no lightening strikes him dead, and the earth does not open up and swallow this person who has "broken the rules." (Even though the self-talk was absolutely *certain* that some earth-stopping disaster *would* happen.)

With more successes, the results are the following:

- Self-esteem
- Freedom
- Clarity
- Joy
- Confidence

The experience of personal freedom and power over one's own life are not easily forgotten. A person who starts living healthier patterns just won't settle for the old painful ways anymore.

## Recognize Common Triggers

We talked about triggers in "Triggers" on page 42. The following are the five most common types of triggers that cause many of our emotionally stormy times. Any one of these triggers is enough, but they are often experienced in combination:

- Relationship problems
  Conflicts with family, friends, coworkers, boss

- Transitions
Any life change, *even good ones*

- Stuffing grief
When the pain of loss, past or present, is repressed instead of grieved, it can lead to depression and/or addictive behaviors.

- Loneliness

- Negative self-talk or beliefs

Learn to recognize these types of stressful events. Leave yourself extra time and space to deal with the additional stress. A helpful tool is the word HALT:

- Hungry
- Angry
- Lonely
- Tired

If you take inventory of your body and discover any of these components active, that's probably not a good time to make any major decisions in your life. You won't be thinking straight. This gives yourself permission to wait until you've eaten, rested, etc.

If a person has situations that trigger feelings of being overwhelmed, out of control, and confused, that does not mean the person is a bad person. Triggers are good, in fact, for providing valuable clues about where there are opportunities for change and healing. What *is* important about triggers is what the person does about it: pretend there is not a problem or look at them as opportunities for change.

## The *Real Me?*

Negative self-talk may develop into negative states of mind. Examples of this self-talk are the following:

- I am a loser.
- Everything always goes wrong for me.
- I have to do everything myself.

- I can't trust anyone.
- I will never have enough.
- I am just a depressed person.
- I am too stupid to get anything right.
- I am weak and helpless. I cannot take care of myself.
- I am just an angry person. I can't change the way I am.

If this self-talk happens often enough, these negative states of mind become one of our "selves." ("Selves" are defined in "Will the Real Me Please Stand Up?" on page 71.) It feels as though "That is just the way I am." As though the destructive self-talk is our very personality and identity.

The truth is, though, that this negative "self" is just a rut our brain got stuck in after so many years of thinking the same thoughts. We can get rid of this fake self without losing who we really are. In fact, getting it out of the way will make room for us to become our real selves.

## Does Changing My Thoughts Really Matter?

A simple study by Mark George, MD, answers this question.[1] He did brain scans on ten normal women while they were thinking different types of thoughts.

| When they thought neutral (not happy or sad) thoughts | Their brains stayed the same. |
|---|---|
| When they thought sad thoughts | Each woman's limbic system (the Security Crew part of the brain) became very active. |
| But when they thought happy thoughts | The activity in the limbic system cooled down. (The conscious, rational part of the brain has more control when the limbic system is calm.) |

# Saying No

---

Handout L
Refusing and Requesting

*Refusing Requests*

A verbal no with a nonverbal yes equals confusion: ensure your body language is complementary rather than contradictory.

How do you know when you want to say no? Listen carefully; check what your body is telling you. Is it a sinking or rising feeling?

*Be clear . . .*
If no doubt, ask for more time or more information.

*Be direct . . .*
Ensure that you use the word "no" in the sentence.

*Be honest . . .*
Avoid making long-winded excuses or blaming others; use a simple explanation where appropriate.

*Be firm . . .*
Set limits, recognizing them as yours, and that other people's limits will be different.

*Be equal . . .*
Acknowledge the right of the person to be upset by your decision. Be sure to emphasize that it is the request that is being rejected, not the person.

Remember

Saying yes when you want to say no means short-term gain but long-term pain.

*Making Requests*

Being assertive involves taking care of our own needs as well as those of others. State directly what it is you want or need. Hints and insinuations merely confuse people.

Remember

Take a risk and ask for what you want; it is worth it!

This is reproduced with permission from *Assertiveness: A Practical Approach*, by Stephanie Holland and Clare Ward (Speechmark, Bicester, 1990).

## Assertive Rights Charter

# HANDOUT I
## The Rights Charter

 HAVE THE RIGHT TO BE
TREATED WITH RESPECT
AS AN EQUAL HUMAN BEING

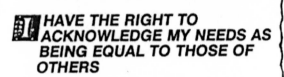 HAVE THE RIGHT TO
ACKNOWLEDGE MY NEEDS AS
BEING EQUAL TO THOSE OF
OTHERS

HAVE THE RIGHT TO EXPRESS
MY OPINIONS, THOUGHTS AND
FEELINGS

HAVE THE RIGHT TO MAKE
MISTAKES

HAVE THE RIGHT TO CHOOSE
NOT TO TAKE RESPONSIBILITY
FOR OTHER PEOPLE

 HAVE THE RIGHT TO BE ME
WITHOUT BEING DEPENDANT
ON THE APPROVAL OF OTHERS

© 1990 S Holland, C Ward & T Whitbread
You may reproduce this page as necessary for instructional use.

---

Handout I
The Rights Charter

*I have the right to be treated with respect as an equal human being.*

*I have the right to acknowledge my needs as being equal to those of others.*

*I have the right to express my opinions, thoughts, and feelings.*

*I have the right to make mistakes.*

*I have the right to choose not to take responsibility for other people.*

*I have the right to be me without being dependant on the approval of others.*

---

Reproduced with permission from *Assertiveness: A Practical Approach*, by Stephanie Holland and Clare Ward, (Speechmark, Bicester, 1990).

# Skill Building

Participants will role-play and process interpersonal styles in a variety of ways, including processing the interpersonal styles questions listed on page 65.

## Summary

By understanding some basic interpersonal styles along with your personality profile, you will be prepared to expand and add more tools to you communication "tool belt."

## Communication Tool Belt

- Observation (page 129)
- Thoughts (page99)
- Self-talk (page99)
- "I" statements (page 116)
- Feedback (page 148)
- Attentive listening (page 135)
- Empathy (page 116)
- Wants (page 148)

## Key Terms

| | |
|---|---|
| Aggressive Behavior | Aggressive behavior is acting in a manner that allows a person to try to get what he or she wants no matter what the cost to anyone else. A person who uses aggressive behavior may feel angry or frustrated. Aggressive behavior includes threatening, accusing, fighting, and attacking behavior. |
| Arousal Level | A change in a person's arousal level means that the person is either concentrating more or concentrating less; his or her attention is either more focused or less focused. With a change in arousal level, a person's physiology is either more or less ready to respond to stimuli in the environment. |
| Assertive Behavior | Assertive behavior is acting in a manner that allows a person to try to get what he or she wants but does not violate the rights of others. An assertive person often gives people feedback about how their behavior is affecting him or her. For example, "When you cut in line in front of me, I get very angry." Assertive behavior can also mean planning a course of action and sticking to it. An example of this could be, "I'm wondering if there's a way for both of us to succeed here?" Assertive behavior is a skill that a person can use, but the use of the skill will not always produce what the person wants. |
| Believability Check | A believability check is a process in which a group member receives feedback about what he or she has self-reported. This provides an opportunity for the group members to see how his or her self-perceptions fit with how others see him or her. Believability checks can have a tone of playfulness or one of seriousness. |
| Nonassertive (Passive) Behavior | Passive behavior is acting in a manner that allows other people to get what they want at the expense of oneself. Sometimes a person who uses passive behavior may feel |

| | |
|---|---|
| | helpless or out of control. Passive behavior includes waiting, receiving, and enduring without resistance to what others impose. Sometimes a person who acts passively becomes angry and then acts aggressively in an effort to regain control. |
| Passive-aggressive Behavior | Passive-aggressive behavior is acting in a manner that allows a person to try to get what he or she wants by indirect, subtle means. A person who uses passive-aggressive behavior may feel angry, but he or she also may feel helpless. Passive-aggressive behavior is an indirect effort to control others and is sometimes difficult to interpret. Passive-aggressive behavior includes sarcasm or unkind words, procrastination and dawdling, and/or inefficiency or forgetfulness. All of these behaviors are indirect expressions of hostility, indirect ways of resisting authority, or indirect means of controlling others.<br><br>Passive-aggressive behavior is more common than either passive behavior or aggressive behavior. It is sometimes very subtle and appears more socially acceptable than aggressive behavior. |
| Self-confidence | Self-confidence is a result of a process through which individuals develop a sense of control over themselves and, to some degree, over the environment.<br><br>Self-confidence usually develops as a person<br><br>• learns skills to help get what he or she wants,<br>• learns skills to cope with situations where his or her needs cannot be met,<br>• puts those skills into practice,<br>• and has some successful experience with those new skills. |

# Chapter 4

## Addiction to Experience

*Wisdom is the most important thing; so get wisdom. If it costs everything you have, get understanding.*

*—Proverbs 4:7*

---

Goal

- To impart the idea that addiction has many faces and individuals may become addicted to experiences related to specific activities, not just to experiences provided by the use of alcohol and/or drug use

- To teach you the biological basis for addiction and to recognize that addiction may start as a behavior

Objectives

- To increase knowledge such that you will be able to describe one model of addiction

- For practical application of the model, you will understand how a person may be addicted to something other than a drug

- To self-evaluate your own potential for addiction and recognize how much of your behavior is automatic versus how much involves conscious choice.

---

- To examine potential dependency, you will be able to identify your individual pattern of addictive experience overtime

- To measure your relationship and adaptability patterns

## Definitions

## Addiction

Addiction comes from the Latin word *addictus*, meaning "given over, one awarded to another as a slave."

> In current usage, addiction means the process through which one comes to depend physically, psychologically, emotionally, or socially upon a very limited set of options to handle his or her life.

For example, a person may depend upon alcohol or other dysfunctional behaviors to the point that it interferes with personal, family, social, and/or occupational functioning. To this person, alcohol / dysfunctional behavior has become his or her major coping strategy to the exclusion of everything else. It is possible to be addicted to almost anything. Even codependency falls into this category. If a substance or an experience meets the conditions of preventing other options and interfering with personal, family, social, or occupational functioning, the term "addiction" may apply.

When a person is addicted to an experience, he or she chronically or compulsively seeks out that experience especially during anxiety, boredom, loneliness, other kinds of discomfort, and sometimes during elation or excitement. The person then, consciously or subconsciously, molds thoughts and behavior around the valued feelings and experience. This increasing attachment to a single object or action serves to prevent the individual from developing other strong lifestyle interests. Everything else—whether the activity is work tasks, eating, running, meditation, drinking alcohol, using other drugs, codependent behavior, or any other—revolves around the person's need for a particular experience. These kinds of behaviors usually provide an initial pleasure followed by a negative emotional state (a high followed by a low). The negative emotional state then is the trigger for repetition of the behavior, which will again provide pleasure.

Repetition of the specific behavior, and in some cases just thinking about the behavior, causes changes in nerve cells in certain pathways of the brain until the person is satisfied. The more rapidly the nerve cells fire, the more intense the experience. The slower the rate, the more relaxed and detached. Individuals will repeat whatever behavior will produce the desired feeling.

## Homeostasis

Homeostasis is a process through which a balance is achieved and maintained even when something happens to disturb the balance. Each person has an automatic self-regulating system that keeps the continuous internal bodily processes operating at the level required for health. One example of this is when starting to exercise, the heart automatically accelerates to supply working muscles with blood. As exercise ends, the heart automatically reduces its rate. A sign of a potential problem comes when the heart takes a long time to slow down. Another example is that as a person becomes overheated, the blood vessels in the skin expand, whereas when cold the vessels contract.

## Set-point

Set-point is the value maintained by an automatic control system (homeostasis). It refers to the actual position or location of the individual's balance. An example of this is body weight. With the intake of food and nutrients, in the context of an individual's level of activity and metabolism, a particular weight is maintained with minimal fluctuations.

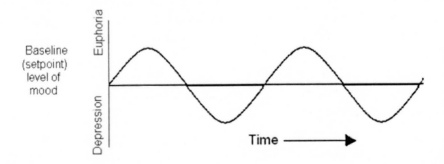

The assumption here is that all systems—physiological, psychological, and interpersonal—seek a state of balance through a homeostatic process. The individual's baseline or ordinary level in each system is the set-point.

With mood states, individuals maintain their usual baseline (set-point) level, above and below which their ordinary moods fluctuate. Most people have moderate ups (euphoria) and downs (depression) and do not intervene drastically in their cycles. On the other hand, some individuals alter their moods through the use of alcohol, other drugs, food, sex, exercise, or other behaviors that cause a change. The frequency, extent, and consequences of mood alteration are the data for understanding how the individual becomes addicted to an experience. There are four ways to voluntarily alter biological set-points: exercise, relaxation, prayer, and drugs.

## Susceptibility to Addiction

List the areas of your life that you would label as possibly addictive.

_____

_____

_____

_____

_____

_____

## Relationship Questionnaire

Check box if answer is yes.

☐   1.   My relationships often involve people who need my help or who are somehow dependent on me.

☐   2.   When I feel I've helped someone, I experience a "high"—a sense of success.

☐   3.   It is important to be needed.

☐   4.   I often find myself "in the middle" giving advice, counseling others.

☐   5.   On occasions, people have become angry when I have tried to help.

☐   6.   I seem to know when bad things are about to occur.

☐   7.   I spend a lot of time thinking through or replaying scenes, trying to figure out what I can do to effect desired outcomes.

☐   8.   I seem to have difficulty starting and maintaining healthy relationships.

☐   9.   It's difficult for me to receive praise or care from others.

☐   10.   I do not like to let myself get angry. When I do, I often lose control.

☐   11.   It's difficult for me to say no.

☐   12.   It is difficult for me to ask for things that I need (work, home, family).

☐   13.   I often over commit my time or over promise myself.

□ 14. It is hard for me to act silly, have fun, and relax.

□ 15. If I'm not productive, I feel worthless.

□ 16. It's difficult to believe that someone could truly love me.

□ 17. I am afraid of really allowing myself to love.

□ 18. I am afraid of being abandoned or being alone.

□ 19. Sometimes I think I expect to be hurt.

□ 20. I find it easy to criticize and blame others.

□ 21. I seem to justify or make excuses for others' actions when they have hurt me.

□ 22. When I know a relationship is about to end, I will stay in it. I will stay in it until I can begin another dependent relationship.

□ 23. It is easy to make me feel guilty and accept blame. I will take responsibility for others. Somehow, things end up being my fault.

□ 24. I am not sure what normal life really is.

□ 25. I often take a stand in a relationship and then go back on what I said I would do. It seems as though I get sucked in again and again.

□ 26. My circle of friends seems to have diminished.

□ 27. I am not aware of what I want. I ask others what they want.

□ 28. I tend to be sick a lot. I can't seem to fight off infections.

□ 29. There never seems to be enough time to do things just for me; things I would enjoy doing.

## Adaptability Patterns

Complete the following evaluation as candidly and honestly as you can. Select the answer that best fits you, and write its number on the line:

In general, the pace at which I do things such as walking and talking is

1   faster than most other people

2   about the same as most other people

3   slower than most other people                         _____

When I am in a situation where I have to wait,

1   I am often uneasy and anxious to get going again.

2   sometimes I am uneasy, other times I am relaxed.

3   I generally remain relaxed.                            _____

Regarding personal achievement,

0   I constantly drive myself to work harder in order to measure up to my own high standards.

4   I sometimes pressure myself to work harder in order to measure up to my own standards.

5   I am relaxed, and I believe I am responding appropriately to my circumstances.                          _____

When I am working within a tight schedule,

0   I am often nervous and frequently become impatient with delays.

2   I am sometimes nervous and occasionally become impatient with delays.

3    I generally remain calm and respond to delays with patience.

_____

When working on tasks that demand concentration,

0    I frequently distract myself with other matters.

3    I have some difficulty staying focused on what I am doing.

4    I usually focus on what I am doing.

_____

In relationships with others,

0    I am highly competitive with others and often resent the successes of others.

2    I am somewhat competitive with others and somewhat resent the successes of others.

3    I am competitive with myself, and I enjoy the successes of others.

_____

When others are speaking to me,

0    I often think of what I want to say next and frequently interrupt the speaker.

2    I listen intermittently, sometimes interrupting the speaker.

3    I usually listen attentively, rarely interrupting the speaker.    _____

With regard to expressing my feelings appropriately in situations,

0    I hide my feelings

2    Sometimes I express my feelings.

3    Most of the time I express my feelings.

_____

In dealing with my deepest personal concerns,

0    I do not discuss my most difficult problems with anyone.

3    Sometimes I have no one to talk with about what is really bothering me.

5    I have trusted persons with whom I can usually discuss whatever is on my mind.           _____

The quality of my sleep is

0    often disturbed by anxious thoughts or distressing dreams

2    sometimes sound, other times disturbed

3    sound, peaceful, refreshing, and undisturbed           _____

When thinking of myself,

0    I often put myself down.

2    I sometimes put myself down.

4    I rarely put myself down.           _____

Regarding my need for information,

0    I am very uncomfortable when I do not know what is going on.

1    I am somewhat uncomfortable with uncertainty.

2    I am usually comfortable with uncertainty.           _____

In my present life situation,

0    I am not the person I want to be and do not do the things I want to do.

2    Sometimes I am the person I want to be, and sometimes I do the things I want to do.

3   I am the person I want to be and do the things I want to do.

_____

When thinking of my life in general,

0   I have regularly thought about ending my own life.

0   I have thought about ending my own life while I was under the influence of alcohol and/or other drugs.

2   I have had none or only fleeting thoughts of ending my own life.

_____

With regard to my personal, social, spiritual, family, and work life areas, my interests are

1   mostly confined to one area

2   somewhat varied

3   numerous and varied

_____

Regarding obtaining rewards for my efforts,

1   I am very anxious about receiving the rewards and recognition I want.

2   I am somewhat anxious about receiving the rewards and recognition I want.

3   I am not anxious about receiving the rewards and recognition I want.

_____

When I evaluate my personal performance,

1   I frequently think I should be able to accomplish a task no matter how hard it is.

2   I occasionally think I should be able to accomplish a task no matter how hard it is.

3   I think I should be able to accomplish a task if it's within my capabilities.   _____

In my present life,

0   I rarely see situations as funny or humorous.

2   I sometimes see situations as funny or humorous.

3   I frequently see situations as funny or humorous.   _____

Regarding my sense of personal responsibility,

1   I rarely follow through on my commitments to others.

2   I sometimes follow through on my commitments to others.

3   I usually follow through on my commitments to others.   _____

I engage in some method of conscious concentration:

0   not at all

2   at least once a week

5   at least once a day   _____

Add up your ADAPTABILITY SCORES and enter the total here.   _____

| Mark your score here | | Your patterns tend to support |
| --- | --- | --- |
| 50 and above | | High Level Wellness |
| 49-44 | | Exceptional Wellness |
| 43-35 | | Average Wellness |
| 26 and below | | Low Level Wellness |

## Stages of Dependency and Addiction

Addiction follows certain stages. It is possible to be addicted to a variety of substances such as alcohol, cocaine, marijuana, coffee, as well as activities or a relationship (codependency) with another person. On the worksheet below, decide on the order of the stages of addiction. Place a "1" to the left of the first stage, a "2" to the left of the second stage, a "3" to the left of the third stage and so on until all stages have been ranked.

_____ Needing the person, substance, or activity to feel normal.

_____ Denying that the substance, activity, or person is hurting one's life when other people point out the problems.

_____ First contact with the substance, person, or activity.

_____ Feeling great pleasure with the substance, person, or activity.

_____ Feeling miserable or uncomfortable when involved with the substance, person, or activity but not willing to let it or him/her go.

_____ Feeling anxious, depressed, angry, or physically ill when the substance, person, or activity is not available.

_____ Friendships, former interest, work, or health suffers because of one's relationship with the person, activity, or substance.

_____ Not acknowledging the faults of the substance, person, or activity.

_____ Believing that the substance, person, or activity will improve one's life.

Answers on page 169.

## Addiction to Experience Continuum

Behavior------- Routine ------- Habit--------- Attachment ------- Addiction

Behavior:    Anything a person does involving conscious action, some activity engaged in once or infrequently, experimentation, an action resulting from a conscious choice. Example: first use of a substance.

Routine:    A regular course of procedure, occurs more frequently than a behavior, usually within conscious awareness.

Habit:    An activity that occurs frequently and may involve little or no conscious awareness. Examples: nail biting, smoking after eating, brushing one's teeth, saying yes automatically (codependency).

Attachment:  An activity to which an individual is personally attached. Mental or physical investment in an activity that, when denied, may result in unpleasant thoughts, feelings, or emotions. Examples: running on a daily basis, drinking coffee every morning, smoking after eating, saying yes automatically (codependency).

Addiction:   A behavior pattern to which a person attaches with compulsion. Self-empowerment is reduced by limiting options or choices. A behavior pattern that interferes with personal, family, social, spiritual, or occupational functioning. Examples: alcohol, sex, tobacco, exercise, falling in love, food, and codependent behavior.

# Dependency Log

Use the worksheet below to track your attachment to any recurring behavior that you observe in your life, whether it is a substance, an activity, or a relationship. Start tracking one week before the workshop.

Item you want to track:

*Example*: Displaying codependent behavior by not being able to say no.

| | Day 1 | Day 2 | Day 3 | Day 4 | Day 5 |
|---|---|---|---|---|---|
| Trigger | | | | | |
| Behavior | | | | | |
| Self-talk | | | | | |
| Feelings | | | | | |
| Strength of Attachment 1 = Weak 5 = Strong | | | | | |
| Times Noticed | | | | | |

# Summary

As you start working on your individual growth, you will be looking at changing behaviors, which will include abstinence, learning to talk and listen in a whole new way, along with a new sense of self-exploration and self-disclosure. "Addiction to experience" starts the thought process as to what role addiction plays in our decision making. A lot of us have developed coping behaviors that keep us from communicating effectively to others. By giving an overview of addiction to experience, we can examine how we can improve our thought processes so we can implement desired healthy outcomes in communicating with others.

## Key Terms

Addiction
Addiction comes from the Latin word *addictus*, meaning "given over, one awarded to another as a slave." In current usage, addiction means the process through which one comes to depend physically, psychologically, or socially upon a very limited set of options to handle his or her life. For example, a person may depend upon alcohol to the point that it interferes with personal, family, social, and/or occupational functioning. To this person, alcohol has become his or her major coping strategy to the exclusion of everything else. It is possible to be addicted to almost anything.

Behavior
A behavior is something that a person can actually see someone do. It expresses external appearance or action. Behavior is sometimes referred to as "observable behavior" just to emphasize the fact that if the behavior cannot be seen, a person cannot be sure what is happening.

Feeling
A feeling is an emotion experienced in one's body. Often, a person experiences a body response before finding words to describe it. As one becomes more self-aware and able to identify body responses when they are happening, one learns to describe feelings quickly.

Homeostasis
Homeostasis is a process through which a balance is achieved and maintained even when something happens to disturb the balance.

Self-talk    Self-talk refers to the conversations that a person carries on mentally about self, about others, and about the environment. A person's self-talk reflects his or her real point of view and beliefs.

Set-point    Set-point is the value maintained by an automatic control system (homeostasis). For example, a thermostat might be set at seventy-eight degrees. A person's weight and temperature are two other examples.

Trigger    Trigger refers to the internal or external cue or set of cues that immediately precede and elicit the substance use or addictive behavior.

# Chapter 5

## Self-awareness Skills:
## Thoughts, Feelings, and Self-talk

*A man without self-control is as defenseless as a city with broken-down walls.*

*—Proverbs 25:28*

*Be careful what you think, because your thoughts run your life.*

*—Proverbs 4:23*

---

Goal

- To examine your present patterns of interacting with others and identify the changes necessary to insure that you are communicating effectively

- To be able to decrease interpersonal misunderstanding and the consequent rationalizations, such as denial, which are frequently associated with drug use, alcohol misuse, codependency, and other compulsive behaviors, by recognizing that self-awareness is enhanced through communication with others

Objectives

- To be able to identify thoughts, feelings, and self-talk in different interpersonal situations as a method of increasing self-awareness

---

- To learn how self-talk can affect your emotions and physiology

- To be able to identify your thoughts, feelings, and self-talk that is occurring in the workshop

- To be able to identify how your self-talk is affecting your behavior in the workshop

## Self-awareness

In order to enhance relations with others, people must first identify what they want to share with others. Although they may frequently want to communicate some information about themselves, they may not know exactly what that information is. Increasing self-awareness is a way to discover this. We create change in our lives by gaining control of our thoughts. We have a choice in determining how we will feel and act.

The apostle Paul understood this. In several places, he reminds us that the hard work of self-control begins in our minds. In 2 Corinthians 10:3-5, he shows us that the battle is not taking place in the physical, external environment. Rather, it is in our minds. We are to "destroy arguments and every proud obstacle to the knowledge of God, and take every thought captive to obey Christ." We are literally to fight against the arguments and irrational reasoning of our minds. We are to capture these thoughts, change them, and bring them into obedience to Christ.

In Romans 12:2, Paul continues with this truth. First, he warns us to "not be conformed to this world," or as J. B. Phillips translates it, "Don't let the world around you squeeze you into its own mold." Don't get caught in the trap of irrational thinking. Don't accept the false idea that your emotions, feelings, and behavior are controlled by the events in your life. Instead, Paul tells you to "be transformed by the renewing of your mind!" He says that you can be changed. And the key to transforming and healing is in the renewing of your mind. Change your thoughts—your self-talk—and you change your life. Occasionally, it is useful to huddle and talk with yourself about what you are experiencing and what you are going to do about it.

## Nine Types of Destructive Self-talk

Destructive and negative self-talk can control how a person sees the world. It blinds a person from noticing any good things. No wonder everything can seem bleak and hopeless when "bad, with no change possible," is the only interpretation the self-talk allows!

When the brain has decided how something is, it looks for evidence to prove to itself that is right. It will twist and interpret observations to make them fit what it has already decided is true. So it is very important to identify what the brain believes and talk back to it as necessary. You can discover what the brain believes by listening to the self-talk and the feelings that go along with it. Here are nine types of "bleak and hopeless" self-talk to watch for:

## 1. I can't help it

There is always something I can do to help myself even in the worst of situations. And maybe there are terrible things going on that I cannot change. But I throw away all the power that I have as soon as I say to myself things like the following:

- If only he had done this differently . . .

- It wasn't my fault that . . .

- I've been so hurt; you can't expect me to . . .

- But she is the one who caused . . .

- We wouldn't have this mess if you would just . . .

- If only . . .

This is called "victim mentality": I am just the helpless victim, and you/they/life are to blame for my problems. As a child, I may have been largely unable to change my circumstances. But now I am an adult, and I DO have power and choices. I can take responsibility for what I do and how I am. But only when

I make the decision to stop thinking like a victim and to start using my power of choice.

It can be terrifying to give up the victim mentality that blames everyone else for my problems. It is very hard to act as an adult instead of being helpless and expecting others to take care of me. I will need the help of friends, a support group, and maybe a counselor to get through this difficult journey into taking responsibility for my own life.

## 2. Negative thoughts only, please

Remember that famous glass of water? Was it half empty or half full? There are always good parts of terrible events and bad parts of the most wonderful occasions. Self-talk that focuses on the negative crowds out the ability to be glad about anything at all. They are like wearing special grey-colored glasses that even take the good parts and make them look bad too!

| Half Full? | The World Through Negative-thinking Glasses |
|---|---|
| It is bright and sunny out. | This glare gives me the worst headache. |
| That was a great dinner. | The tea was so bitter I could hardly taste anything else. |
| Movie tickets are half-price today | at that theater with the hard seats. |
| The children performed beautifully. | Their pink outfits clashed horribly with the red socks. |
| I won the million-dollar jackpot! | All that work to get low-income benefits, down the drain! |

## 3. Have to

Our security crew (the brain) tends to take things literally. And if I say, "I must be cheerful around my mother," it thinks that there are no alternatives. I can never frown, never ask to change something I don't like, never express a wish for something I don't have. After all, "must" means it is fate; there are no other options; probably I will die if I don't do it. Might as well just lock me up in chains, considering how much freedom I feel!

Notice when you start to use the following dangerous words. Stop and pick another phrase instead.

| Dangerous Words | Freeing Phrases |
|---|---|
| Should | I could |
| Must | I want to |
| Have to | If I choose, I can |
| Need to | It would fit with my goals if I |
| Got to | It is in my best interest to |
| Ought to | It would help the situation if I |

## 4. Mind reading

This can be a tough one to catch. Anytime I "know" what another person thinks, feels, or wants, it is time to check for mind reading. Unless that person specifically said what they think, feel, or want, anything that I believe is only my guess. And I need to realize that I am probably guessing wrong, or at least incompletely.

The only way to find out what is true is to check it out with the person. Review "Observations" on page 21 and "Feedback with a Guess" *on* page 118 for how.

## 5. Virtual people

It is OK to observe someone's behavior and say to yourself that you liked or didn't like a particular action. But as soon as you label the whole person something like "jerk," "snotty," "crabby," "irresponsible," (or whatever) you cut off your ability to see that person clearly. Remember how the brain takes whatever it believes and twists its view of its experiences around to meet that belief?

If you call someone a "jerk," then even when he does something kind, your brain will say,

> Boy, I wonder what scam he is pulling now? You got to admit, he puts on a good act at being kind. He almost had even me fooled!

Maybe he is just playing a confidence game. But maybe he isn't really the total jerk you thought. As long as the "jerk" label in your brain controls your interpretations, you will never know, will you?

When a brain decides that another person always acts in a certain way, the brain's picture of how that person is can become so strong that it has a life of its own inside the brain. Just as computer games that seem real are called "virtual reality," the brain's picture of that person becomes a "virtual person." That virtual person can be so large and seem so real that it completely blocks out who the other person really is no matter what they say or do.

Making careful observations of the person's actual behavior and words can bust through the "virtual person" false picture. See "Observation" on page 20 for where to start.

## 6. Always/never

Do you remember the advice the teachers used to give about how to take multiple-choice tests? Answers that say "all" or "always" and those that say "never" are always wrong. (Well, almost always, anyway, but close enough to "always" to make it a good rule.) The same is true in life. Beliefs like the following:

- He always ignores me.

- Everyone will think I am stupid.

- No one will talk to me if I go.

- You never listen to me.

- Every time I try to get better, it never works.

- I always mess everything up.

The problem is, if my Nonconscious Crew (the brain) hears these words from my mouth or my self-talk, it takes them literally. It is not able to stop and analyze "Not everyone will think I am stupid since most people are too busy worrying about themselves to even notice me!" or "When I do try to get better, it does help some. Every little bit helps." No, the Nonconscious Crew believes the always/never talk completely and rushes about in panic at what it must mean. Since it believes "he always ignores me" and "I always mess everything up," the Security Guard will send "Danger, Danger!" signals even if all I want to do is say, "Excuse me, this is my floor," to leave the elevator. Catching those always/never self-talk patterns and replacing them with more accurate beliefs can make daily life much calmer.

## 7. Predicting the future

Predicting-the-future self-talk is similar to always/never self-talk and negative self-talk. It takes very little actual information and makes a Technicolor movie about the bad things that it is sure will happen. Sure, a person should consider what might happen, then make plans to prevent it. But what is damaging is being so controlled by the fear and worry that one cannot experience and enjoy today. When a person worries and imagines what it would be like for something bad to happen, the same stress chemicals get released into the body as if the event were really happening. The damage to one's mental and physical health can be just as great as the damage from a real trauma.

Mark Twain said,

> I have experienced many terrible things in my life—some of them actually happened.

## 8. It's all about ME

The Nonconscious Crew takes in what is happening and uses the best information it has to interpret what the event means. Sometimes, the Nonconscious Crew will take things personally. It takes little events and gives them personal meaning when actually, the events probably had nothing to do with the person. For example:

- She didn't say hello to me this morning. I must have hurt her feelings.

- The waiter put onions on my burger when I always order plain. They are trying to tell me that they want me to stop coming here.

- My daughter got in trouble at school. I should have spent more time with her when she was a preschooler. It is my fault.

- That's the third person today that has talked about someone with an anger problem. It is a sign. I must have an anger problem and don't even realize it.

Many interesting and strange coincidences happen every day, but they have nothing to do with me, and it is unlikely that they are signs about what I should do. If you think that you offended someone or that they are trying to tell you something, check it out with that person. Review "Observations" on page 128 and "Feedback with a Guess" on page 152 for how to ask. And God is fine too with us asking him for more clarity about what he wants and thinks before we make a decision about what to do.

# 9. Believing emotions

Feelings come up for lots of reasons. They are often (very often!) based on powerful events that happened long ago, and something today just happened to stir it up. It is a good idea to pay attention to strong negative feelings and look for an opportunity to work on healing those hurts. It is not a good idea to just believe everything you feel; use feelings as signals. Think about what the feelings are telling you, then look to see if there is any evidence for it. Some examples of feelings that may seem very true but probably have nothing to do with the facts of your life today are the following:

- When I notice that my shoe is unlaced, I feel dumb.

- When no one asks for my help, I feel that no one trusts me.

- When you don't comment on my work, I feel that you're disappointed with me.

- When you smile and greet me so warmly every time I come, I feel that you are just saying you love me just to be nice.

- When I pass out the desserts at an office party, I can feel everyone's eyes on me. They are watching to pounce on any mistake I make.

Strong negative feelings that seem out of proportion to the facts usually indicate a need for inner healing. Talk with your group leader or church leadership about what inner-healing resources they are aware of in your area.

## More on Emotions

Recent advances in brain science find that emotions are the very "thinking medium" of the brain that connect the parts of the brain together. We are primarily emotional creatures with some logic added in. By the way, words play very little part in how emotion is communicated. Facial expression, eye gaze, tone of voice, bodily motion, and the timing of response are each fundamental to emotional messages.[1]

The emotion we operate best on is JOY. The deepest joy is found in the delight of close relationships with people that know me well and are glad when they can be with me. With them, I can share my sad emotions and know they felt them with me and understand. Then we can come back to being glad just to be together, and we all gain strength from that joy.

But sometimes it seems impossible to get in touch with what I am feeling. The Feeling Word List (on the inside back cover of this workbook) is a helpful place to start developing a feeling vocabulary.

The following factors can make it hard to know what my emotions really are:

## Emotions As Signals, Not Facts

True emotions are important bits of information about ourselves. But remember that a sentence that starts "I feel that . . . " is usually about to express a thought or conclusion, not a true feeling.

Remember also that the feeling just tells me that *something* is going on in me, not what it is or if it I am good or bad. Emotions are just information, not something good or bad. (It is our *behavior* in response to those emotions that may be "good or bad.")

---

[1.]   Daniel J. Siegel, *The Developing Mind (Guilford Press, 1999)*, 121.

# Mixed Emotions

I may get confused when my emotions seem to contradict one another. Yet it is normal to feel

- GLAD to see my friend and ASHAMED that I haven't yet paid him back the money I borrowed,

- RELIEVED that she is safe and ANGRY that she was so late,

- and EAGER to be early to the communication workshop and RELUCTANT to attend since I wonder if parts of it will be uncomfortable for me.

# Feelings about Feelings

I can have feelings about having feelings! I may have learned (or decided) that certain feelings are NOT OK to have. When I was growing up, some feelings, such as anger, may even have been dangerous to express. So now, I have *other* feelings about the first feelings. I may feel the following:

- Guilt about feeling proud of myself

- Shame about being angry at my mother

- Embarrassment at how happy I am about a simple "babyish" thing

- Fear at anyone knowing that I am angry

It may be hard for me to identify the original feeling of satisfaction or anger or happiness because I am too busy trying to stuff that feeling out of sight.

But the truth is that feelings are just feelings. They don't mean that I am good or bad. They are just a clue that something is going on in me. For example, if I start getting angry, maybe I have an unforgiveness problem. But then again, maybe too much coffee makes me short-tempered. Or maybe I am coming down with the flu, am worried about my child, or slept poorly last night. The anger just tells me that *something* is going on, but not what.

## Overwhelming Emotions

There are six basic emotions that can be difficult to have:

- Sadness
- Fear
- Shame
- Rage/Anger
- Disgust
- Hopeless despair

(Other difficult emotions are variations and combinations of these six.)

To mature, we need to learn how to cope gracefully with each of these emotions. That is, we need to be able to be feeling the emotion but still act normally. Growing up, we may have only learned how to handle some of these emotions, but not others. Or we may have learned to handle a little bit of a feeling, but not intense versions of it. People either have learned how to handle a feeling or they get overwhelmed and "lose it" whenever that feeling comes up too strongly. For instance, a confident person may suddenly be tongue-tied if they find that they have made a mistake (and are feeling shame). This otherwise-confident person is not able to handle this level of shame, and it triggers a "security alert" (page 41).

The bad news is that we were supposed to learn about handling feelings from our parents but often didn't.

The good news is that even as adults, we can still learn how to handle difficult feelings. When we share our lives, feelings, and experiences with safe people that do well with emotions (and they share their life stories with us), our brains learn from them the emotional skills we missed out on as children. These practical brain skills are only caught and practiced from healthy, committed relationships with other people, not from a book.

## Emotions Are Not Safe to Have

Some children find that their world is chaotic or unsafe. To keep themselves safer, they block out their feelings and live by constantly analyzing their options logically. Unfortunately, that was probably the best option at the time.

It is challenging, then, as an adult, to choose to become aware of those blocked feelings. But it is possible and can lead to a more peaceful and satisfying life. For one thing, when I know what my emotions are, they usually lose power over controlling my behavior. That gives me more choices and control in my life.

## Self-talk Test

Instructions: Place an X on the number that represents how often you currently use a self-talk strategy to unblock your energy and an O around the number to represent how useful you think the self-talk strategy might be for you to try in the future.

When you are stuck, unable to take action, how often do you use these self-talk strategies?

|  | Seldom | | | Frequently | | |
|---|---|---|---|---|---|---|
| 1. Gather more sensory data? | 1 | 2 | 3 | 4 | 5 | 6 |
| 2. Reprogram or reframe your thinking? | 1 | 2 | 3 | 4 | 5 | 6 |
| 3. Revise your expectations? | 1 | 2 | 3 | 4 | 5 | 6 |
| 4. Work through your fears? | 1 | 2 | 3 | 4 | 5 | 6 |
| 5. Reorder your priorities? | 1 | 2 | 3 | 4 | 5 | 6 |
| 6. Expand your comfort zone? | 1 | 2 | 3 | 4 | 5 | 6 |
| 7. Share your self-talk with others? | 1 | 2 | 3 | 4 | 5 | 6 |
| 8. Let go of irrational beliefs or wants? | 1 | 2 | 3 | 4 | 5 | 6 |

List one or two situations where one of these self-talk strategies would be helpful.

Situation               Strategy

Situation               Strategy

## Experience to Pressure

There are times you experience pressure from others, such as peers, supervisors, spouses, parents, and children. Fill out the worksheet below describing from whom you feel pressure (person), what you feel pressured to do (activity), what you usually do, what you would like to do, and how you could change your usual response to the response you would like.

| | |
|---|---|
| Person | |
| Activity | |
| What I usually do | |
| What I would like to do | |
| How I could change my response | |

## Thoughts, Feelings, and Self-talk

Thoughts, feelings, and self-talk contribute to the decisions you make. Thoughts are ideas or opinions that you believe. Feelings are emotions that you experience. Self-talk is the conversation you carry on in your head.

Fill out this worksheet listing your thoughts, feelings, and self-talk in response to each of the situations described. An example is provided below:

| Situation | Initial Thought | Initial Feeling | Ongoing Self-talk |
|---|---|---|---|
| Someone spills coffee all over your desk. | My work is ruined! How could you do this to me? | Tightening in your shoulders | Just great! Now what am I going to do? |
| On your way to your morning appointment, you are delayed by forty minutes due to a traffic accident. | | | |

On the chart below, write down one frustrating situation that comes up again and again in your life. Add your thoughts, feelings, and self-talk.

| Situation | Initial Thought | Initial Feeling | Ongoing Self-talk |
|---|---|---|---|
| | | | |

## Summary

This session lays the groundwork for your being able to identify your internal dialogue and to then notice the relationship of your dialogue to your thoughts and your behavior in different situations. In the workshop, we will process the different forms and test in this chapter and dialogue as a group there outcomes.

# Key Terms

Arousal Level   A change in a person's arousal level means that the person is either concentrating more or concentrating less; his or her attention is either more focused or less focused. With a change in arousal level, a person's physiology is either more or less ready to respond to stimuli in the environment.

Behavior A behavior is anything that a person can actually see someone do. Behavior is sometimes referred to as "observable behavior" just to emphasize the fact that if the behavior cannot be seen, a person cannot be sure what is happening. For example, you think someone is looking at you. "What is the behavior?" "What is the inference?" The behavior is that the person is looking. The inference is that the person is looking at you.

Belief A belief, in its broadest sense, implies that a person accepts something as true whether it is based on reasoning, prejudice, emotion, or authority. A belief usually consists of an object and some characteristic or attribute of the object, such as "all drug users started by smoking pot." A belief usually sounds like a fact or a piece of information.

The important issue is that a belief is something that a person thinks is true. A person will only examine and possibly change beliefs in an encouraging environment that feels safe.

Feeling A feeling is an awareness of an emotion. Oftentimes, there is a physiological sensation associated with a feeling. For example, when a person feels angry, he or she may be experiencing a rapid heart rate, a flushed face, tension in the jaw, or knots in the stomach. Awareness of physiological sensations can help a person describe what emotion he or she is experiencing.

As one becomes more self-aware, able to identify feelings when they are happening, one learns to describe feelings better. Often a person experiences a feeling even before finding words to describe it. Words often seem like a vague and imprecise ways of describing what one feels. With practice, however, it becomes easier to be aware of feelings and to describe them to others.

Self-awareness Self-awareness results when a person examines his or her feelings, thoughts, and behavior. It does not mean that person must change because of this increased awareness. It does mean that one now has information that will allow for a decision to make changes or to continue doing the same thing(s).

Self-confidence  Self-confidence is having a sense of control over oneself and being able to respond effectively to the environment.

Self-confidence is usually developed as a person

- learns skills to help get what he or she wants,

- learns skills to cope with situations where his or her needs cannot be met,

- puts those skills into practice,

- and has some successful experience with those new skills.

Self-esteem  A person with self-esteem respects himself or herself as a person who

- has a wide array of life skills from which to choose,

- is willing to use these skills effectively,

- and is willing to cope when things do not go as planned.

This does not mean that if a person has high self-esteem, things never go wrong. It does mean that no matter what happens, the individual will use skills that are appropriate to get through the situation.

Self-talk  Self-talk refers to the conversations that a person carries on mentally about self, about others, and about the environment. A person's self-talk can be consistent or inconsistent with what other people have actually said. Sometimes a person receives praise ("Good job!") and turns it into criticism ("But he didn't notice where I really screwed up the job. If he saw that then he wouldn't have said that I did such a good job. He would think I am as sloppy as the rest of the crew."). There can be a big difference between what was said and the individual's self-talk about it. How a person feels in a situation depends largely on what label he or she has assigned to it. Restructuring one's self-talk can change a person's overall experience of a situation as well as initiate the process of behavior change.

# Chapter 6

# The Language of Self-responsibility ("I" Statements)

*What this adds up to, then, is this: no more lies, no more pretense. Tell your neighbor the truth. In Christ's body we're all connected to each other, after all. When you lie to others, you end up lying to yourself. Go ahead and be angry. You do well to be angry—but don't use your anger as fuel for revenge. And don't stay angry. Don't go to bed angry. Don't give the Devil that kind of foothold in your life.*

*—Ephesians 4:25-27 (The Message)*

---

Goal

- To learn that you create your own communication behaviors, both verbal and nonverbal

- To recognize that others use those behaviors to determine the meaning of what I say

- To communicate responsibility and effectively by learning and practicing, taking ownership for all that you say in the remainder of the workshop

- To recognize the inaccurate assumptions you can make with people and the various guesses you can entertain yourself with because of those assumptions—in other words, is what you see always what you get?

---

Objectives

- To be able to identify the difference between an observable behavior and an inference (guess) as a way of distinguishing facts from perceptions

- To practice making "I" statements as a way to demonstrate personal responsibility and the skill of respect

- To practice "checking out" the validity of your assumptions of others as well as the group as a whole

## Responsibility for Self: "I" Statements

Taking personal responsibility (using "I" statements) in any group environment is paramount to the safety and respect of others. It's also a more direct approach, which leads to getting to the point instead of talking around the point.

Responsible people speak for themselves. This is known as the skill of *respect*. They are self-aware; they recognize their perceptions as their own and identify their experiences as their own. At the same time, they leave room for others to see and experience things differently by letting others speak for themselves. This is also *respect*.

The "I" statement is the core skill of assertive communication. In it, I tell what my truth is and let other people have their own truths. I show respect to others by not trying to control them or get them to think the way I do. I show respect for myself by identifying myself as the owner of my ideas. To do so states that I am a person worthy of having my own thoughts and opinions. I can care about what other people think without thinking any less of myself. I can listen carefully to others' opinions, wants, and feelings without being controlled by what they say or the way they say it. Let's take a look at how we do this.

# When . . . I Feel

The "I" statement starts with an observation, then states feelings or self-talk.

Observation + feelings or thoughts = "I" statement

So the basic pattern of an "I" statement is,

- When (this happens) I feel . . .

   or

- When (this happens) my self-talk is . . .

| Communication Styles | "I" Statements |
|---|---|
| When people go to scary movies, there are problems sleeping at night. | When *I* see skeletons and corpses in a movie, *I* feel agitated, and *I* don't sleep well that night. |
| It's important to choose greeting cards carefully. | When *I* get a birthday card, *I* feel good if the message is friendly. Sometimes *I* feel offended at those joke cards. |
| Even though I work from home, this is still *my* office. Don't touch anything on my desk! | When *I* sit down to work, *I'm* already feeling pressured by the responsibility of earning a living. Then when something is missing from my desk, *I* feel out of control and panicky. |
| I can't work another day with that boss![1] | When he tilts his head like that and smiles and tells me what a competent worker I am, then hands me someone else's unfinished work, *I* feel furious and unfairly treated. |

| | |
|---|---|
| Huh? What on earth do you mean? | *I'm* talking slowly right now and having a hard time following because *I* feel so tired. |
| Can't you give a man a moment's rest? What is it around here, a zoo? | When *I* come home from work and even the neighbor kids are running through our house and slamming doors, *I* feel tired and irritable. *I* would like some quiet rest before spending time with the family. |
| Not everyone is that competitive, you know. | When *I* play volleyball, I really enjoy being with my friends. *I* don't care if we win or lose. |
| Oh, thank you so much for the flowers! | Thanks! When *I* get flowers, *I* feel appreciated. |
| Whatever everyone wants to order is fine with me. | When *I* am at a Chinese restaurant, *my* self-talk is that others might not like what *I* order. |

## I Am in Charge of Taking Care of Myself

"I" statements can feel strange and uncomfortable to start using. Sometimes it feels rude or selfish to just come out and say what I feel or want. But which is better:

- tell my friend what I want up front

or

- stew inside later because she chose something that I didn't like?

Part of taking responsibility for myself is not expecting others to read my mind. If I don't tell them, they can't know for sure what I feel and want.

## Points to Consider

When people demonstrate personal responsibility by speaking for themselves, they

- identify themselves as the creators of their thoughts, feelings, and actions;

- show respect for others;

- leave room for others to be self-responsible;

- and add to the accuracy and quality of their communication.

## Observations

*Sensory data* is the impressions received by the senses: sight, hearing, touch, taste, and smell. The brain automatically receives all the incoming information and decides what is important for you to notice. It just filters everything else out. The brain may not direct you to notice the dust on the furniture or the warmth of the sunbeam coming in the window; but, boy, the kid with muddy feet on the white carpet sure gets your attention! The part that you consciously notice (the kid and the exact quantity of mud) is your *observation*.

You can train your brain to let more of the sensory information through its filter and into your conscious awareness. You just have to let the brain know what kind of information you want to become aware of. You train it by regularly and deliberately focusing attention on the types of details and information you want to be noticing.

The more you notice, the more you know.

The more you know, the better choices you'll be able to make.

The better your choices, the more control over your own life.

## What to Notice

A sailor trains himself to notice the height of the waves, the direction and speed of the wind, the flow of the currents. A skillful communicator can learn to "read the waters" too. Some communication "undercurrents" to focus on the following:

Facial Clues

- Eyes open, closed, narrowed

- Direct eye contact or looking about

- Mouth shape

Body Clues

- Shoulders back or hunched

- Posture slouched or erect

- Breathing rate

- Arms crossed, waving or quiet in lap

- Hands open, clenched, pointing, clutching a pencil, making small movements

- Legs crossed, stiff, or restless

- Feet tapping, squirming, or tucked under

Sight Data

- Space—how close you are to one another. "In your face",or at a comfortable distance

- Clothing—neat, tailored or haphazard, formal or casual

Sound Data

- Voice—loud, soft, mumbling, clearly spoken

- Pace—rapid speech, slow measured words, halting

- Tone of voice—apologetic, decisive, strained, confident

- Speech inflections—strong statements, hesitant statements that sound like questions

## Another Observation versus Self-talk Test

What do you notice about the people in the cartoon below? Thoughts like, "He is bored" and "She is in love," probably pop quickly into your head. That is the brain's Nonconscious Crew at work, quickly sorting out the incoming mail (what you see and sense) and telling you what is important and what it means.

But what body clues caused you to believe that he is bored and she is in love? What are the observations behind the conclusions about these folks?

Be like that detective that wants "just the facts, ma'am" so he can consider carefully if his conclusions are correct. Look at the observation clues and know what your conclusions are based on.

## Label the Label

Labels are wonderfully helpful. If a can is labeled "Green Beans," I can be confident that it does not contain any pineapple slices. If I ask for "Total Lawn Care," I can expect a green lawn, but not a new roof. If my friend says his boss "went ballistic," I picture the boss yelling, threatening, maybe throwing things. Labeling is putting a name on objects ("Green Beans") or actions ("Total Lawn Care" or "going ballistic") that quickly conveys what it is about. A label is a sort of shorthand way of saying *my opinion* about the situation.

A problem with labels comes, though, when the other person has different definitions of what the labels mean. Maybe he grew up eating "green beans" of a mushy, overcooked brand (mixed with pineapple chunks) that tastes nothing like the crisp but tender variety I like. So when I say the peas he cooked me are as good as green beans, he thinks I hate them. Maybe my friend grew up in a very emotionally controlled home, so when the boss scowls and speaks quietly about what changes need to happen, my friend gets frightened about the scowl and labels that as "going ballistic." Many misunderstandings, arguments, and hurt feelings are nothing more than a result of having different meanings for the same words and not realizing it.

A part of taking responsibility for my own thoughts, feelings, and communication is to prevent this type of misunderstanding by

- making detailed observations

- and identifying when I am labeling.

Notice in the following examples how much more clearly understood the *observation and a label* version is and which communication style would it be easier to *hear* without getting defensive or hurt.

| Communication Styles | Observation and a Label |
|---|---|
| These peas you cooked me taste really bad. | These peas you cooked me are dry and unseasoned. I label you a *bad* cook! |
| My boss went ballistic today. I just don't know how I am going to stand the stresses at work! | When my boss read our quarterly financials, he sat without talking for several minutes with a stony face. Then he scowled and typed off some fast e-mails. He made a couple of phone calls, and he talked so loudly you could almost hear the words through his closed door! I label his behavior *insensitive*. I feel so tense I don't know what to do. |

| Give me my money back on these bananas. I will never shop at such a fruit fly haven store again. | The top bananas in the bag were yellow, but most of the ones underneath were black with split skins and pulp oozing out. I label this store as *unclean*. I want a refund. |
| --- | --- |
| Hey, son, you're finally getting it! | Son, when you put the food back in the frig and wipe off the breadboard after you make lunch, I label you as *responsible*! |

## Definitions

Observation. An account of what physically happened. Other people can agree that the observation is true even if they don't agree about why it happened or what the person really meant. It does not have other emotional baggage attached to it. Example: "He yelled, rolled his eyes, and danced around."

Label. A distinctive name for a general type of situation or behavior. It is the speaker's opinion and identification of a particular observed behavior, and it may or may not be true. A label often brings up pictures, feelings, and self-talk in the hearers mind. Example: "When I see you running out in the street with your eyes closed, I label you as crazy."

Remember that taking responsibility for communication means letting others know which parts are my opinions and interpretations. The trick with using labels responsibly is to

- realize the difference between observations and labels,

- provide an observation to explain the label,

- and identify when you are about to use a label.

Some phrases that can identify a label are the following:

- When . . . I label that as . . .

- When . . . I call that . . .

- When . . . I tell myself that . . .

- When . . . my self-talk is . . .

Using labels can be appropriate as long as the label is identified as being my own label (that is, my own opinion), and I explain it with an observation. If I say,

> When you tease the cat by holding out the food then pulling it away (OBSERVATION), I label that as *cruel* (LABEL),

the hearer can understand that I am talking about the way the cat is being treated. I am not rejecting his whole person. The hearer will find it easier to not get defensive or be deeply hurt, so he is more likely to think clearly about his treatment of the cat. (And he just might even decide to change his behavior!)

A problem arises, however, when blanket labels are put on people without observations to show which specific behavior the label refers to. A blanket label, such as

> you're cruel (LABEL, but based on what?)

says that every single action that person does is cruel with no hope of ever being different. This type of blanket label usually provokes feelings of being criticized or stifled and does not encourage better and more open communication. See the following examples:

| Inappropriate Labeling of People | Responsible Labeling |
|---|---|
|  |  |
| I am a clumsy oaf! | Boy, when I hit that table coming around the corner too fast and knocked the milk shakes all over my hostess, I call that a *clumsy* move! |
| You're always so nice. | When you answer my questions so patiently, I don't feel stupid anymore and label you as *nice*. |
| You're so cruel. Stop putting me down! | When I hear you say I'm stupid, I tell myself that you're out of control, and I'm labeling you as *cruel*. |

Note also that it is just as important to not label myself as it is other people. People are just too complex to fit into one label. (And unlike a can of green beans, people can change.) A worse result of labeling is that when my self-talk puts a blanket label on a person (even if I don't say it aloud), the label keeps me from seeing and thinking clearly about the person. See "Virtual People" on page 102.

## Importance of Not Judging

When "I" take ownership for labeling someone, it takes the edge off judging them. If I say you're crazy, and I *don't* take ownership for the label (I message) and *don't* include an observation, I'm not communicating effectively. So when I just say you're crazy, I'm leaving out some pretty important information.

This is what an effective labeling should sound like: "When *I* see you run out in the street between on coming traffic speeding in both directions, I get fearful for you, and I'm labeling you as *crazy*."

What I just communicated was I saw something he did (running into speeding traffic), and I took ownership for my feelings (I get fearful), and I labeled him as *crazy*.

Nobody likes to be labeled as crazy; however, if they have more information as to why I think the way I do, and I share and take ownership for those feelings, I stand a much better chance of having the other person hear me and receive what I'm saying without feeling judged. Once you can master communicating in this fashion, the easier conflict resolution becomes.

## Group Activities

### Process

- The group will practice using "I" statements in a variety of ways in order to experience how the new language feels.

- The group will practice checking things out (observation, sensory data) with other individuals and the group as a whole.

## Speaking Skills—Quiz Yourself

Instructions: Identify the main speaking skill in each statement below.

1. Speaking for Yourself
2. Describing What You Observe
3. Label Your Feelings
4. Expressing Your Thoughts

Answers

1. I get angry and frustrated when you don't follow
   through with what you say you will do.          _____
2. You don't even care.                            _____
3. Wow, I'm excited to hear your voice!            _____
4. I assume you are going with us tonight.         _____
5. I didn't see the game last week.                _____
6. I noticed your leaning back in your chair, not smiling.   _____
7. I think you misunderstood me.                   _____
8. I'm thinking about taking the trash out in a minute.   _____
9. My confidence is running high.                  _____
10. My confidence is running high, and I feel excited!   _____
11. I heard you sigh when I called your name.      _____
12. My main desire is to finish school.            _____

Answers: (1) 1 and 3; (2) 4; (3) 3; (4) 4; (5) 1; (6) 2; (7) 4; (8) 4; (9) 4; (10) 3 and 4; (11) 2; (12) 4

## Communication

Awareness of self may enhance communication with others because much of what is being shared gives others information that otherwise would remain hidden and unclear, inept and misunderstood.

Over the past thirty years, behavioral scientists have carefully studied the process of human communication and have discovered that certain behaviors yield more predictable outcomes. Specific behavioral skills and processes enable people to send messages more accurately, effectively, and efficiently. Furthermore, studies indicate that the people who learn to resolve conflicts and differences through effective communication skills training and usage have less stress and are more prepared to be at peace with themselves and others.

## Nonverbal communication (team building)

The manner in which participants say things, have facial expressions, and have body languages are more often used by others to determine meaning than the actual words. This is supported by the following statistics that say that communication can be broken down as follows:

- 7% verbal

- 38% nonverbal

- 55% interpretation

Think about and describe the different nonverbal elements of communication. The following, among others, are relevant:

- Position: physical placement in relation to others in the room

- Posture: orientation of head and orientation of body (i.e. slumped or erect)

- Gestures: movement of hands, head, legs, arms (i.e. nodding, squirming and scratching, face touching, swallowing, moistening of lips)

- Facial expression: eyes (stares or looks away), mouth (frowns or smiles), eyebrows (raises or lowers)

- Vocal nonverbals:

  1. Intonation: tone of voice

  2. Volume: the loudness or softness of a person's voice

  3. Rate at which a person speaks

  4. Trailing off at the end or not finishing sentences

# Observation to Inference (Guess)

People frequently make interpretations about someone's personality or private life based on clothing, jewelry, hairstyle, physical size, and so forth. Because the inferences are usually made quickly and unconsciously, people may not bother to determine the accuracy of their judgments by checking them out with the other person. In the same way, certain behaviors, such as stereotyping, interfere with people really getting to know one another. Effective communication requires each person to look beyond outward appearances. People can increase the effectiveness of their communication by becoming aware of how often they act on their inference without checking them out and without determining whether these inferences are based on actual observations or on stereotypes.

> Modeling effective communication is to make an observation and attach a guess or an assumption to the observable behavior you're seeing and to check it out with the other person.

Example: "When I see you scratching your head, I'm *guessing* you didn't understand what I just said. Does that fit for you?

In the workshop, we will practice modeling the above example. Use the following form on page 100 to list some of the reoccurring events that you deal with on a weekly basis. We will process as a group exercise to practice how to communicate these items in a new way.

As a guide, remember the following for sending clear messages:

Skill No. 1 Speaking for Yourself

Speaking for yourself identifies you as the source of your message.
Speaking for others produces resistance.
Over-responsible "You" statements creates resistance.
Under-responsible, speaks indirectly, lacks congruency and substance.

Skill No. 2 Describing What You Observe

This skill chronicles the linking of observations to interpretations.

Skill No. 3 Labeling Feelings

With this skill, you state what you are experiencing emotionally and actually label the emotions/feelings. Use the feelings list provided in this book.

Skill No. 4 Expressing Your Thoughts

This is the skill of saying what it is you are thinking, believing, assuming, or expecting.

## Observation to Inference

People make assumptions (inferences) about the meaning of other people's behavior. In this exercise, observe other group members. Write down four observations (i.e. facial expressions, body language, tone of voice, statements made, actions) and write down two possible inferences for each observation.

| | |
|---|---|
| Observation 1: | Inference 1a: |
| | Inference 1b: |
| Observation 2: | Inference 2a: |
| | Inference 2b: |
| Observation 3: | Inference 3a: |
| | Inference 3b: |

| Observation 4: | Inference 4a: |
| | Inference 4b: |

---

## Speaking Skills—Exercises

---

## Old and New Ways of Speaking

Instructions: Write out a sentence or two that illustrates and contrasts how you would tell a particular person about what he or she does that irritates you. The old way is the way you've spoken in the past. The new way is using "I" messages, giving observation detail, sharing feelings, and labeling the observable behavior.

Old Way

New Way

A Complete and Concise Message

Instructions: Formulate a message, in twenty-five words or less, using the four speaking skills used in the quiz.

Speak Another Person's Language

Instructions: Develop a message you must communicate to another person using the four speaking skills used in the quiz.

---

## Summary

---

This session addressed the importance of taking responsibility for oneself by giving you a chance to experience the impact of using "I" messages when dialoguing with the group. We also looked at aspects of nonverbal communications and observations to a guess. This sets us up very nicely for the remainder of the workshop when more group interaction will be encouraged.

# Key Terms

| Arousal Level | A change in a person's arousal level means that the person is either concentrating more or concentrating less; his or her attention is either more focused or less focused. With a change in arousal level, a person's physiology is either more or less ready to respond to stimuli in the environment. |
|---|---|
| | |
| Congruence | Congruence is the matching of experience, awareness, communication, and behavior. Congruence may refer to the matching of verbal communications and nonverbal behavior; the matching of what a person states are his or her values and his or her actual behavior. |
| | |
| Control of Communication | The principle of control of communication concerns the individual's style of interaction with others. Some elements include the loudness of voice, the actual words chosen to convey the meaning, along with some other more subtle behavior such as facial expression and body posture. Control has two requirements: that one actually means all elements of the messages sent and that the total message is direct. |
| | |
| Denial | Denial is a restructuring of perceived internal or external conditions in order to change thoughts, experiences, or actions. Frequently, the motive is to reduce the impact of or to avoid expected consequences. For example, when a person demonstrates incongruity between what is being said and facial and other nonverbal behaviors, the likelihood is that a process of denial is occurring. |
| | |
| Economy of Expression | This principle of communication is demonstrated when the individual says no more or no less than needs to be said to convey the meaning. Talking around a point, not getting to the point, or in any way preventing the hearer from understanding the meaning are all ways in which people violate this principle. |
| | |

| "I" Statements | Too often, a person speaks for other people when he or she is speaking for only himself or herself or when wanting to say something for himself or herself. For example, "You're not making any sense to me," instead of "I feel some confusion about what you are saying." "I" statements mean taking ownership of one's thoughts and feelings and making the ownership public. One way to do this is to start the sentence with "I" and then finish it with how one feels or what one believes. |
| --- | --- |
| Inference | An inference is an interpretation, a judgment, or an assumption that a person draws from observable behavior. |
| Label | A descriptive word or phrase applied to a person or group as a convenient generalized classification. A label reflects that person's particular perception and may not match another's perception. |
| Self-disclosure | Self-disclosure is a skill whereby a person tells others about current or past thoughts or feelings. A person may feel more vulnerable and see oneself as taking a larger risk by self-disclosing thoughts and feelings about one's present experience than he or she would about disclosing past events. Self-disclosure involves taking ownership for thoughts and feeling through the use of "I" statements.<br><br>In an effort to enhance communication and relations with others, a person may want to consider the appropriate time to self-disclose, where an appropriate place might be, and who an appropriate person might be with whom to self-disclose. |

# Chapter 7

## Self-awareness Skills: Responsibility for Interaction (Listening)

*Let everyone be quick to hear, slow to speak and slow to anger; for the anger of man does not achieve the righteousness of God.*

*—James 1:19-20*

---

Goal

- To give you an opportunity to examine your present communication listening patterns

- To make necessary changes for better communication, including ensuring that you are respecting and caring about the other person by listening to their story in an uncontaminated way and that you are understanding their experience accurately so as to discover useful information and increase the chances of arranging outcomes you would prefer

Objectives

- To demonstrate effective listening skills during the listening experience

- To pursue understanding without necessarily agreeing or disagreeing, without promoting or defending hour own experience, and without jumping to conclusions

---

- To get to the core of issues faster with less interpersonal stress

- To gain uncontaminated, quality information

- To encourage continued disclosure

---

- To reduce fear and defensiveness—our own as well as others—and increase trust and disclosure

- To relate more constructively when it is your turn to talk to others' legitimate concerns

- To earn the right to be heard after you have listened to others tell their story in full

- To save time later by not having to return to issues to clarify misunderstandings and mop up poor communication decisions

- To create a collaborative atmosphere for generating new agreements based on current understanding

- To leave others feeling good about you and themselves, which will nurture understanding and safety

- To feel good about your own caring behavior and that of others'

## Points to Consider

Be prepared:

Sometimes, those of us in our emotional dysfunctions find it very hard to get outside of our own hurts, habits, and hang-ups to listen to others effectively without having a hidden agenda or negative self-talk.

Active and attentive listening is a learned skill that is an extremely important ingredient to successful communication with various groups and our significant relationships, not to mention how it enhances teambuilding, counseling, facilitating, teaching, and general career development. Be prepared to be coached a lot by your facilitator for the remainder of the workshop.

## Why Active Listening?

Have you ever seen the old movies where the captain is on lookout, directing the ship's progress? The dialogue goes something like this:

> Captain: Five degrees to port.

> Pilot: Port five degrees.

> Captain: Engines full speed.

> Engineer: Full speed ahead.

Do these sailors have such boring conversations all the time? No, only when they want to be sure of staying in the safe shipping lanes and not being hulled by a reef. They would rather have these foolish and boring conversations now than later have to say, "Nine degrees? Oops, I thought you said twenty-nine degrees to port. Better break out the lifeboats."

These sailors are practicing a simple form of active listening. They first listen attentively to the other, then repeat back the details in their own words. Active Listening takes care that the first person's statements are accurately heard before moving on to a response. This shows respect to the speaker, helps them feel less fearful and defensive, and encourages the speaker that it is safe to tell more. It is also the best chance you have of getting clear information from them and understanding where they are coming from. And a more complete understanding of their point of view will help you together come to choices, agreements, and compromises that you are both happier with.

When we, landlubbers, do our first active listening exercise, a common response is "this is stupid." Repeating back what someone just said when I know perfectly well what they mean is embarrassing and uncomfortable. It feels childish. There, I've said it for you. So now, go ahead and try the following active listening exercises. Instead of focusing on how "foolish" you feel repeating back what your partner said, watch your partner's face and body language as they realize you really listened and understood them. How many relation-ship reefs would you like to avoid?

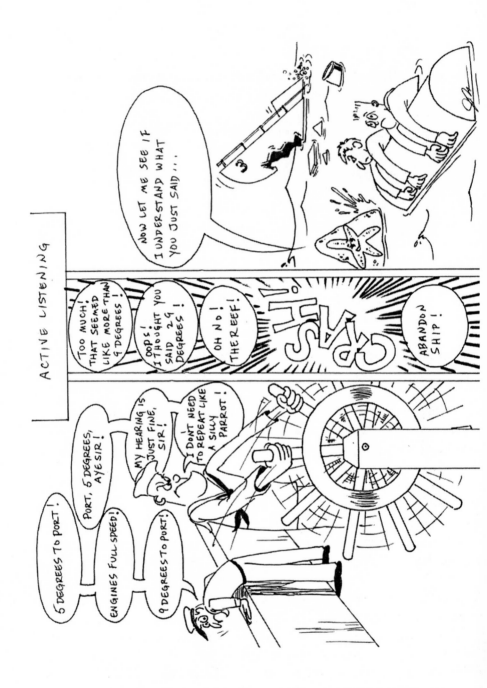

**Self-Awareness Skills: Responsibility for Interaction (Listening)**

## Listening Skills Breakdown

Listening is the key for understanding others and building strong relationships. Three dynamics are involved in each relationship: *rapport, control,* and *trust.*

# Three Types of Listening

These include selling yourself listening, control listening, and attentive listening.

# Selling Yourself Listening: Wanting to Lead

You listen briefly and then interrupt to disagree, give advice, or sell your perspective to the other person.

# Control Listening: Wanting to Clarify

You use questions to control the direction of the conversation.

Four kinds of Control Questions include the following:

1. Why questions
2. Leading questions
3. Closed ended questions
4. Multiple questions

# Attentive Listening: Wanting to Discover

This type of listening helps gain an overview, understand, deal with "what is," and connect with others.

Let's look at the skills involved with the listening cycle:

Skill No. 1 Looking, Listening, Monitoring Congruencies

This skill involves establishing rapport—matching to create rapport—and tracking dialogue and attitudes.

Look and listen for opportunities to service the other person. Just like a good customer service representative would do.

Skill No. 2 Acknowledge Messages

Validate what the other person says at different junctures even if you don't agree. I don't have to agree; however, when I acknowledge the other person, I'm telling them that what they say has value.

Skill No. 3 Invite More Information

Ask for more information in a user-friendly way even when you don't want to.

Skill No. 4 Gaining Understanding and Clarifying

Asking open-ended questions (in a user-friendly way) and checking out your interpretations.

Checking out body language for congruence or mixed messages.

Skill No. 5 Summarizing—to Ensure Accuracy of Understanding

This process guarantees understanding by summarizing the essence of the message. Paraphrase what you actually hear. Focus on the speaker's message. Don't rebut.

Summarizing shows understanding and punctuates a conversation.

## Practice Skills at the Next Opportunity—Exercise

Action Plan:

To practice gaining awareness at the next group function you attend.

1. Observe how the group communicates. What styles are being used, if any?

2. What is not being used, and how is it affecting the meeting?

3. Watch for incompleteness.

After the meeting has gone on for a while, experiment with the above skills.

After the meeting is over, assess your skill level. Ask yourself if you used all the above skills. What skills do you need to work on? Keep a journal of future meetings to assess your progress and outcomes.

1. What skills did I use?

2. What was the outcome of using each skill?

3. What skill do I need to practice more?

4. On a scale of 1-10, 10 being the best score, what number would I give myself on each skill?

5. Who can I share this with?

6. What do I need to do next to become a more effective listener?

## Active Listening and Fast Food

The active listening cycle is like placing an order at a drive-through:

| Step | Waiter | Customer |
|---|---|---|
| 1. Listen | May I take your order? | Three burgers and fries. |
| 2. Repeat | You want three regular hamburgers and an order of fries? | |
| 3. Right? | Is that right? | Yes. |
| 4. Is there more? | Will there be anything else? | No, that's it. |

For a fast-food chain, millions of dollars of profit depend on accurately hearing what the customer wants and maintaining good customer relationships. You can bet that they stick with the most proven techniques! Shouldn't that work well for the rest of us too?

## Active Listening, Step by Step

### First, just listen

"Just listen" doesn't mean go on vacation. "Just" listening is hard work. It means looking at the person and listening carefully. "Just" listen, instead of

- analyzing what is wrong with what they believe,

- agreement or disagreement,

- thinking that they shouldn't have those feelings,

- planning how to defend yourself from what they are saying.

Just listen to/for understanding

- what they believe,

- how they see the situation,

- how they feel about it,

- what they want,

- and what their face and body tell you about their feelings.

Active listening is just that—listening without interrupting. Even asking too many questions can disrupt the speaker's train of thought. You may, however, interrupt and ask, "May I repeat back what you have said so far before you go further? I don't want to lose the details."

### Then repeat

After that crucial first step of listening attentively and quietly, it is time to check and see if you understood. Repeat the main points of what they just said. You can use your own words but keep it accurate to what they really said, not what you think they should have included. In touchier situations, stick to using their very words as well.

## Is that what you meant?

Be sure to get some sort of acknowledgement that what you repeated is accurate before you move on. They may smile, nod their head, or say, "Yes." If there is not very clear acknowledgement, you need to ask, "Is that right?" or "Is that it?"

## No, what I said was . . .

Of course, if they say that you didn't hear what they meant, listen again. After they explain more, again you try to repeat it until they are satisfied that you really heard them.

## Is there more?

After asking if you repeated it back correctly, PAUSE! Pause to let them know that you are willing to wait for them to think about their answer. Otherwise, if they feel rushed, their self-talk may be, "I have maybe five seconds left of her attention, then my time will be up. I'd better just get the important points in fast and hide the parts I feel more emotional about."

Pausing to wait for a response is a powerful statement that says, "I am really ready to listen." It invites deeper sharing than what the person previously may have felt would be safe.

## My turn

After the other person agrees that you heard accurately what they said, then it is your turn to share your viewpoint and have the other person mirror it back.

## Choose to Lead or Follow, to Talk or Listen

- Every interaction between two or more people contains leading and following behaviors.

- Leading involves talking and asking questions.

- Following involves using effective listening behaviors.

- Most people would rather lead (talk) than follow (listen).

- Most people also want to be listened to and understood accurately.

## Listening

Perhaps the most important factor in effective communication is listening. Listening is a prerequisite for responding, but it is sometimes taken for granted or considered an inconvenience. Frequently, a person is not listening at all when another person is talking but is busy focusing on and formulating their upcoming reply. This lack of attention deteriorates the communication process.

Most of us have habits, which keep us from paying full attention to the talker when there is a stressful or complicated issue. At other times, as we listen, we mainly evaluate what the other person is saying. We form judgments about whether it is right or wrong, good or bad, or whether we agree or disagree. We compare our own viewpoint with the other person's. Our behavior is more reactive then attentive, and we find it easy to interrupt—whether by statements or questions. When we listen in these ways, we keep ourselves front and center and focus our attention more on our own experience than on the other person's.

The way in which a person listens is a message in itself. Others in the communication process will notice how well they are being heard. The goal of listening is understanding. When a person understands, he or she is able to see the expressed idea from the other person's point of view, to sense the other person's feelings, and to grasp that person's frame of reference.

> Good listening puts your own concerns on hold temporarily and encourages others to be the leader—to tell his or her story spontaneously and without your interference.

Your goal is understanding—without necessarily agreeing or disagreeing, blaming or defending, or jumping into action (posing a solution). Most good coaching, mediation, or counseling skills require great listening skills

Listening involves

- focusing full attention on what the other person is saying;

- recognizing the feelings, underlying attitudes, and beliefs;

- and paying attention to nonverbal behavior, voice tone, and word choice.

Listening demonstrates interest in the speaker, builds rapport and respect, and helps to prevent misunderstanding and its consequences.

Additional guidelines for effective listening include

- paying attention to the content of what is being said;

- attending to nonverbal behavior;

- listening for meaning, not just words;

- suspending attitudes and biases;

- and not interrupting.

The common blocks to effective listening are

- judging and evaluating messages prematurely, agree/disagree;

- allowing distractions such as noise, time of day, one's work, or topic to interfere with listening;

- asking questions or developing response before the speaker has finished;

- and analyzing to solve problems or find answers for the speaker.

## Unexpected Benefits of Active Listening

Many times, when a person wants to talk about a bothersome issue, a friend or spouse will interrupt with good advice and ways to fix it. The friend or spouse cares and feels pressure to make it better. But usually, all the person really wanted was to be listened to and understood! Friends and especially spouses can show they care by practicing active listening. As an added benefit, the friends or spouse get the added benefit of not pressuring themselves to try to come up with a fix for something they probably have little or no control over. After all, which is easier active listening or actually solving the problems?

## Problems with Active Listening

Active listening can be a painful and difficult habit to acquire since listening to another's pain can trigger my own issues. When someone I care about shares frustrations, pain, or problems, I may feel weighed down by the responsibility to make it better. I may feel their pain as my own if I was never taught how to be compassionate without being crushed by others' pain. Or I may fear that I will be blamed as the cause of the problem, especially if it is a family member talking. If issues like these make active listening difficult, it becomes a good opportunity to seek inner healing. See "Soul Wholeness—the Big Picture" on page 116 for more resources.

Sometimes, listening to another's opinion, and especially when I repeat it back, feels as though I am saying that I agree with it and that I approve of them thinking that way. Or I am afraid that if I repeat back what they say they feel and believe, but I don't say how wrong it is, it means I have to start feeling and believing that too. That when I just repeat back what they say, I am saying about myself that I am as mixed up or as bad as they are. But in fact, if I repeat back another's opinion without judging it, I am saying about myself that I am a person that can respect other's opinions enough to listen before I answer.

## Real Life

You may be the one talking and wondering if the person listening to you really heard what you said. You can request some active listening by saying, "I would feel better that you understood me if you would tell me what you think I just said. OK?" You cannot control how they respond to this request, but by asking, you have done what you can to take care of yourself.

# Workshop Skill Building Exercises

• Workshop groups will practice a variety of roles to develop the skill of active listening.

• The skill may be incorporated into possible role-plays and various group interactions.

• You will be coached to use the skills learned throughout the remainder of the workshop.

## Summary

The point of listening is to gain information and improve the communication process. In practicing the skill of listening, the participant can increase awareness of how he or she stops self from listening effectively.

Key Terms

Behavior         A behavior is something that a person can actually see someone do. It expresses external appearance or action. Behavior is sometimes referred to as "observable behavior" to emphasize the fact that if the behavior cannot be seen, a person cannot be sure what is happening.

Feeling          A feeling is an emotion experienced in one's body. Often, a person experiences a body response before finding words to describe it. As one becomes more self-aware and able to identify body responses when they are happening, one learns to describe feelings quickly.

Listening        Listening describes an open process in communication that calls for

                 • paying attention with one's body (putting down one's work, leaning toward the person, and making eye contact;

- paying attention with one's words (repeating parts of what the person has said, asking questions to gain understanding);

- and showing understanding of words and feelings.

Self-awareness

Self-awareness results when a person examines his or her feelings, thoughts, and behavior. It does not mean that a person must change because of this increased awareness. It does mean that one now has information that will allow for a decision to make changes or to continue doing the same thing(s).

Self-talk

Self-talk refers to the conversations that a person carries on mentally about self, about others, and about the environment. A person's self-talk reflects his or her real point of view and beliefs.

# Chapter 8

## Awareness Skills:
## Responsibility for Interaction
## (Feedback)

*Every man shall kiss his lips that giveth a right answer.*
*—Proverbs 24:26*

*It is an honor to receive a frank reply.*
*—TLB*

*He is a true friend who is honest with you.*
*—Moffatt*

*An honest answer is a sign of a true friendship.*
*—GN*

*A straightforward answer is as good as a kiss of friendship.*
*—NEB*

Goal

- To increase the information you have about how you come across to other people

- To discover how your behavior impacts others, thereby increasing your self-awareness

- To encourage risk taking in using the skill of giving and receiving feedback

Objectives

- To use the guidelines provided in this session to give feedback to other group members during this session as well as during the remainder of the workshop

- To be able to understand and resolve issues more effectively

- To gain confidence in sharing thoughts and feelings

- To interact with group members at a higher level of genuineness

- To label feelings in an accurate way and self-disclose to the other person or group

## Feedback

Feedback is communicating information to a person about how the person appears to or affects other people. It is a way of answering the questions "Who am I to others?" and "How do I affect others?" As a result of feedback, one may consider whether or not to change behavior, which may be inconsistent with his or her intentions. Feedback increases one's awareness of self and one's effect on another person's thoughts and behavior. It also helps to clarify relationships and to promote understanding. Feedback is a means of demonstrating self-disclosure and making observations of others.

Feedback always uses an observation and an "I" statement. Feedback tells the other person what my reactions are to their words or actions. By starting a feedback statement with a detailed observation, the hearer is more likely to understand why I have certain feelings or self-talk. By utilizing an "I" statement, I take ownership and model self-disclosure. By stating what I observe in detail and owning it (using "I" messages) and labeling a feeling or thought, the chances are better that the hearer will be able to receive the communication without feeling as defensive or attacked.

*Feedback is the breakfast of champions.*
—*Author Unknown*

*The right word spoken at the right time is as beautiful as gold apples in a silver bowl.*
—*Proverbs 25:11*

*A word spoken at the right time is like a secret which has been whispered in the ear and it stands out like a design of gold set in silver.*
—*GN*

Here are some examples of what feedback might sound like:

## When you . . . I Feel / When you . . . I Tell Myself . . .

| Other Communication Styles | "I" Statements |
| --- | --- |
| How do I know where the money went? | When you scowl and ask me questions about our finances, *I* tell myself I must have spent too much, and *I* feel *ashamed*, so *I* get *defensive* and clam up. |
| You are easy to work with. | When you call and tell me when you will be late, *I* feel *appreciated*. |
| You could tell someone how you feel sometimes, you know, instead of ignoring me! | When you get quiet and won't tell me how you are doing, *I* feel *rejected* and afraid. |
| You get me so mad I can't see straight. | When you keep forgetting to empty the garbage, my self-talk says that you don't really care about me, and *I* get *angry*. |
| I can't talk right now. | When you call in the late afternoon, *I* am always rushed and *stressed*. I would like a chance to chat; let's agree on another time to talk. |
| You shouldn't snap your gum. It's so rude. | When you keep snapping your gum, *I* start to feel *irritated* and *nervous*. |

| You love that computer more than you do me. | When you spend more than an hour every night on chat rooms, *I feel jealous.* |
| Can't you slobs even rinse a dish out and put it in the dishwasher? Why should I shop and cook and clean for you? | When I go to cook dinner and discover a kitchen-full of dirty dishes, *I feel resentful.* My self-talk is that I don't want to cook for you anymore. |

## Why Taking Responsibility Works

Taking responsibility for my own thoughts, feelings, and communication means that when I state a feeling or opinion, I take ownership by saying it is mine ("I" messages). When I say that this is *my* opinion, the other person may feel less pressure to agree with it or be controlled by it. Some phrases that identify the thought as my personal interpretation are the following:

- When . . . I feel . . .
- When . . . my self-talk is . . .
- When . . . I tell myself that . . .
- When . . . I call that . . .
- When . . . I say to myself . . .
- When . . . I'm thinking that . . .

This is called owning the thoughts and feelings. It is saying,

> Hey, this is what's going on in my head. Maybe it's not true, but it's what is real for me.

It helps the hearer understand me with less chance that the hearer is put on the defensive or feels a need to argue. When I give a detailed observation, I'm only saying that it is what *seems* to be true based on what I'm seeing through *my eyes.* It gives the hearer room to navigate as they become more aware of their own behavior. It models to him that I will listen respectfully if he shares his own thoughts and feelings—his own truth.

Taking responsibility for my communication also means that I use the most detailed and complete observations to back up the thoughts, feelings, and opinions I express. Then the hearer doesn't have to guess, and probably guess wrong, about what may have caused me to say what I said. He doesn't have to wonder what I might be upset about or what he did wrong. The hearer can follow my logic and see what my ideas are based on. He has a better chance of understanding what I am really saying and feeling without feeling attacked.

## Feedback Can Help the Hearer

Have you ever seen a comedy in which the main character has done some big goof like having a big stain on the back of his shirt or food in his teeth or accidentally cutting off half of his hair, but he doesn't realize it? He goes through the show wondering why people are acting so funny, but nobody tells him what is wrong. They may call him a "goofball" and "crazy" and "irresponsible" and "insensitive," but he doesn't have any idea what the problem is unless someone specifically points it out.

We all have occasions in life like this poor character who can't see himself for what he looks like to others. It is a kindness to give people careful observations and a feedback.

> I'm feeling a bit nervous for you because I'm noticing black pepper in your teeth before your important meeting. Can I help in any way?

At least now he has a chance to see himself from another perspective and perhaps choose to change his behavior (clean his teeth).

## Guidelines

Guidelines to Giving Feedback:

- Use "I" statements.
- Comment as soon after the behavior as possible.
- Describe specific, observable behaviors.
- Do not use guesses or assumptions.
- Give feedback that is appropriate to the situation.

- Include a request if appropriate.
- Avoid blaming others.

Disclosing our feelings openly and honestly can enhance the quality of all our relationships.

Remember: the following formula is one way that feedback can be expressed:

> When you did/said (describe a specific behavior), I felt/thought (describe how you felt or what you thought).

Guidelines to Receiving Feedback:

- Acknowledge the feedback.
- Ask for clarification if needed.
- Listen to the other person.
- Be receptive and nondefensive.
- Ask for feedback if you want it.
- Avoid rationalizing or overgeneralizing. (Defend)
- Decide how to use the feedback in an effective way.

## Feedback with a Guess

> *The glory of kings is to search out a matter.*
> —*Proverbs 25:2*

> *The mind of the prudent is ever getting knowledge, and the ear of the wise is ever seeking—inquiring for and craving—knowledge.*
> —*Proverbs 18:15, Amplified Version*

## What's a Guess?

A guess is one kind of self-talk (see "Self-talk," page 98). When I am trying to figure out what an observation means (see "Observations," page 128), I come up with some sort of answer. The answer I come up with is probably not based on complete information, so it is really a guess[1].

---

[1]    Guesses are often called "inferences."

Our brains have special circuits that analyze another person's face, voice tone, and body position, and tell us what the other person is feeling. This is called "mind sight." This analysis going on inside the brain may also tell us what the other person wants or what they really mean (but are not saying). Brains can actually do a very good job of this. In fact, the brain's analysis of what another person feels or wants is so often correct that we forget that it is also often NOT correct. And those times that we misjudge what the other person feels or wants can cause BIG problems. If you hear people trying to patch up a relationship with phrases like, "But I thought you wanted . . . " or "But I thought you *liked* it when . . . ," then you know that they are trying to fix the problems caused by "mind sight" mistakes.

Would you like to prevent BIG problems? Have smoother relationships? Base decisions on more complete and accurate information? Using feedback with a guess is the tool to use to double-check your conclusions BEFORE you act on them.

## When You . . . I Feel . . . and I Am Guessing That You . . .

"Feedback with a guess" starts with a "feedback" (page 118) and then states what I am guessing about what the other person is feeling, wanting, or thinking. It is expressed in a way that invites the other person to respond and clarify their feelings or intentions.

Observation + My feelings or Thoughts + Guess
= Feedback with a Guess

The guess does not have to be accurate, but is really an invitation for the other person to share more. A careful feedback and a guess shows the other person that you care because

- your observation shows that you paid attention to them in the interaction,

- sharing your feelings shows that a personal relationship is important to you,

- and the guess says that you are wanting to better understand the other person.

## Examples of Feedback with a Guess

| Other Communication Styles | Feedback with a Guess |
|---|---|
| Wow, thanks a lot! | Look at the careful coloring and neat printing on this birthday card. I feel special that you made your own card for me. I'll bet you worked pretty hard on this! |
| I hate it when you treat me like that! | When you rolled your eyes at me and said I was stupid, I was feeling disrespected and attacked. My guess is that you are having a bad day? |
| Thanks. About time someone did some cleaning around here. | With the carpet vacuumed and all that clutter gone, I feel more relaxed coming home. I'm guessing you're exhausted! |
| I can't stand it when you act like that! | When you call me a liar, I feel discounted and blamed. My guess is there is something additional you are not telling me? |
| Good game, champ! | Boy, when you walloped that last pitch, I was thrilled. Then you were scowling on third, and I thought you were pretty torn between staying safe on third or running home? |

## Using Feedback and a Guess during Discussions

People often talk about the facts but leave out what they feel and want. Somehow, the person still seems unresolved. Notice if they have included any feelings in their statements. Ask, "When you . . . I am guessing that you feel . . . ?" The sense of connection and being understood may be the missing piece that has prevented the other person from feeling satisfied with the interaction. Asking, "When you say . . . I am guessing that you want . . . ," may also be appropriate.

Remember, this is a time to connect with where they are, not to try to get your viewpoint across. That can come later.

# Skill Building

In the workshop, you will have an opportunity to practice giving and receiving feedback in a variety of settings and situations. Please use the feelings list (on the back cover) frequently.

## Summary

It is important, in our one-on-one relationships as well as the various group environments we are involved with, for individuals to take responsibility for their responses to others' behaviors.

> Your feelings and thoughts are not dependent on what happens "out there," but rather upon what response you choose to have about what happens "out there."

Feedback can be labeled as hard to give, "When you shouted, I was feeling caught off guard and fearful," or a warm fuzzy, "When you were sharing deeply and crying, I was applauding inside and I felt more connected to you." Feedback is a hard skill to develop because of our potential fears of sharing our feelings and emotions to another person. Developing this skill moves you to a deeper level of sharing.

Key Terms

| Behavior | A behavior is something that a person can actually see someone do. It expresses external appearance or action. Behavior is sometimes referred to as "observable behavior" to emphasize the fact that if the behavior cannot be seen, a person cannot be sure what is happening. |
|---|---|
| | |
| Economy of Expression | This principle of communication is demonstrated when the individual says no more or no less than needs to be said to convey the meaning. Talking around a point, not getting to the point, or in any way preventing the hearer from understanding the meaning are all ways in which people violate this principle. |
| | |

| | |
|---|---|
| Feedback | Feedback is any information that a person has received that lets him or her know how others perceive him or her.<br><br>Feedback should<br><br>   •   describe a specific behavior,<br>   •   occur as soon as possible after the behavior,<br>   •   and deal with one situation at a time.<br><br>The following formula is one way that feedback can be expressed:<br><br>When you did/said *(describe a specific behavior)*, I felt/ thought *(describe how you felt or what you thought)*. |
| Feeling | A feeling is an emotion experienced in one's body. Often, a person experiences a body response before finding words to describe it. As one becomes more self-aware and able to identify body responses when they are happening, one learns to describe feelings quickly. |
| | |
| "I" Statements | Too often, a person speaks for other people when he or she is speaking only for himself or herself or when wanting to say something for himself or herself. For example, "You're not making any sense to me," instead of "I feel some confusion about what you are saying." "I" statements mean taking ownership of one's thoughts and feelings and making the ownership public. One way to do this is to start the sentence with "I" and then finish it with how one feels or what one believes. |
| | |
| Self-awareness | Self-awareness results when a person examines his or her feelings, thoughts, and behavior. It does not mean that person must change because of this increased awareness. It does mean that one now has information that will allow for a decision to make changes or to continue doing the same thing(s). |
| | |

| Self-talk | Self-talk refers to the conversations that a person carries on mentally about self, about others, and about the environment. A person's self-talk reflects his or her real point of view and beliefs. |
|-----------|--------------------------------------------------------------------------------------------------------------------------------------------------------------------------------------------------------|
|           |                                                                                                                                                                                                      |

# Appendixes

## Assertive Body Language

### Handout F
### Body Language

© 1990 S Holland, C Ward & T Whitbread
You may reproduce this page as necessary for instructional use.

This is reproduced with permission from *Assertiveness: A Practical Approach*, by Stephanie Holland and Clare Ward (Speechmark, Bicester, 1990).

## Handout C
## Behaviour Types

© 1990 S Holland, C Ward & T Whitbread
You may reproduce this page as necessary for instructional use.

Reproduced with permission from Assertiveness: A Practical Approach,
(c) Stephanie Holland & Clare Ward, Speechmark, Bicester, 1990

This is reproduced with permission from *Assertiveness: A Practical Approach,* by Stephanie Holland and Clare Ward (Speechmark, Bicester, 1990).

## Books and Other Rresources

*The Life Model: Living from the Heart that Jesus Gave You*
By Friesen, Wilder, Bierling, Koepcke and Poole
Shepherd's House, 1999
Order from *www.care1.org* or call CARE at 231-745-4950
This eighty-three page book is packed with information, insights, and wisdom about how relationships, therapy, and various support environments must work together for effective recovery and Christian maturity. A must-read for Christian recovery leaders.

*Attachments: Why You Love, Feel, and Act the Way You Do*
Clinton and Sibcy
Integrity Publishers 2002
Explains how the relationship patterns learned in the first few years of life generate our present feelings, self-talk, and behavior patterns (unless changed by effective recovery work). Fairly easy reading with many true-life examples.

Theophostic Prayer Ministry
*www.theophostic.com*
A prayer methodology that asks the Holy Spirit to reveal the source of specific harmful self-talk and belief patterns, then invites Jesus Christ to communicate his truth and love into that area of memory. (Not to be confused with the New Age philosophy of a similar name.)
Call 270-465-3757 to find a minister in your area.

*Change Your Brain, Change Your Life: The Breakthrough Program for Conquering Anxiety, Depression, Obsessiveness, Anger, and Impulsiveness*
Daniel G Amen, MD
Three Rivers Press, 1998
This book is more involved reading, but only because it has so much information. It has many practical exercises about how to change self-talk as well as specific advice about using herbs, nutrition, and drugs to help brain functioning.

*Assertiveness: A Practical Approach*
Stephanie Holland and Clare Ward
Winslow Press
Available in the United States from WPS Creative Therapy Store
12031 Wilshire Blvd, Los Angeles, CA 90025
1-800-648-8857
Many practical exercises and examples of how to deal with life more assertively. The publisher kindly allowed us to reproduce several of their handouts in this workbook.

*Victory over the Darkness: Realizing the Power of Your Identity in Christ*
Neil T. Anderson
*www.ficm.org*
This short book talks about finding (and living) our real self instead of destructive negative identities.

*Safe People: How to Find Relationships That Are Good for You and Avoid Those That Aren't*
Dr. Henry Cloud and Dr. John Townsend
Zondervan Publishing House
Finding the right group of people to get close to can be hard work. Just because people can say the right words doesn't mean they are healthy on the inside. This book talks about which behavior patterns identify the safe people that you want to be connected with and the unsafe ones to keep some distance from.

*www.christianrecovery.com* has recovery resources, links to specific recovery programs, and some wacky humor. You might be able to track down recovery groups in your area via some of their program links.

Communication training programs
See the following Web sites for training locations and dates:

*www.communication-empowerment.com*
*www.prepinc.com*
*www.couplecommunication.com*

# Support Group Goals and Expectations

Adapted from Bill Morris, *The Complete Handbook for Recovery Ministry in the Church* (Thomas Nelson, 1993).

1. To be safe for one another, group members

   1. maintain confidentiality at all times;

   2. do not minimize, criticize, judge, or condemn what another member may be thinking, feeling, or doing;

   3. do not permit direct confrontation or physical or verbal attacks;

   4. do not attempt to fix other people's situations, give advice, take other's inventories, or tell others how to work their recovery programs;

   5. and follow the established format, guidelines, and principals.

2. To accept one another, group members

   1. listen attentively with open minds and hearts to whatever others share;

   2. ask questions only to clarify and understand;

   3. affirm one another whenever anyone takes the risk of sharing and being honest;

   4. encourage one another to change, grow, and overcome;

   5. identify and relate to one another's successes and failures;

   6. model recovery and are willing to sponsor others in their recovery;

   7. remind one another to be patient with the process of recovery and to be gentle with themselves and their mistakes;

8. do not interrupt or enter into side conversations while others are speaking;

9. do not determine what others think, feel, or need without checking it out with them;

10. and do not interfere with the expression of painful feelings.

3. To be responsible for ourselves, group members

1. speak only from personal experience;

2. are committed to keeping the focus on ourselves and our recovery;

3. speak the truth honestly and appropriately;

4. are willing to risk being honest, vulnerable, and trusting of others and God in order to change and grow;

5. put awareness and acceptance into action to take steps to recovery;

6. remain humble and teachable, being open to insight and wisdom from others and from God;

7. accept that God's timing is individual and perfect;

8. do not try to fix one another or solve one another's problems;

9. do not try to convict or change on another's behavior'

10. and do not blame others or circumstances for our problems, realizing that to do so makes us victims and leaves us powerless.

# Support Group Covenant

To encourage a high level of trust, love, and openness in my support group,

I, _____, covenant with my group's members to do the following:

> I agree to make attendance at all group meetings a top priority for the period of which the group meets. During these weeks, I will choose this group first when making decisions about my priorities and my time. If I must be absent, I will contact my group facilitator or leave a message with the church office at—.
>
> I will commit to my time each week to complete the appropriate unit of study in workbooks before the group session.
>
> I agree to make every effort to be on time for this support group program beginning at—pm, recognizing the importance of the entire program, including worship, which softens my heart for the healing the Lord wants to work in me. Upon dismissal, I agree to go directly to my small group, understanding that I hurt myself and other group members when I am late.
>
> I agree to stay until each meeting is adjourned. I recognize that I affect the dynamics of the group in a negative way if I leave early. My desire to leave early may be an expression of my unwillingness to face up to the feelings I am feeling in response to what is happening in the group. If I must leave the meeting early, I will explain my reasons to the group before I leave. I will be open to discussing my early departure at the next group meeting.
>
> I agree that what takes place in the group is CONFIDENTIAL. If I break my commitment to confidentiality, I understand that I may be asked to leave the group.
>
> I agree to do everything I can to help create an atmosphere of trust in the group.

I will be patient with other group members as we allow God to work in each of our lives. I will not try to give advice or to pressure other group members to do what I think best.

I will inform my group leader of any physical or emotional problems that might arise through my participation in the group.

I agree to be supportive of other group members as they struggle with their emotions. When needed, I will encourage other group members with the words, "I support you."

I agree to engage in rigorous (not brutal) honesty toward myself and other group members (1 Corinthians 13).

I agree to let other group members confront me in love so that I can grow.

I agree that if for some reason I decide it is necessary to leave my group during the period of time in which the group is meeting, I will discuss it with my group so there is some closure. I will not just stop coming!

Signed _____ Date _____

# Answers to Exercises

## Identifying Feelings (page 27)

These are some of the possible feelings that could be associated with the original "I feel" statement. You may have thought of others.

| "I feel" | True Feeling? | Actual Feelings |
|---|---|---|
| Angry | Yes | |
| Hurt | Yes | |
| Rejected | Yes | |
| That I'm a loser | No | disappointed, rejected, frustrated, confused |
| Unloved | No | Rejected, hurt, depressed, disappointed |
| That I can't do anything right | No | frustrated, |
| Doomed | No | discouraged, depressed, beaten down |
| Overwhelmed | Yes | |
| Crazy | No | confused, rejected, bewildered |
| Out of control | No | panicky, tired, hungry, dizzy, desperate |

## Stages of Dependency and Addiction (page 93)

5     Needing the person, substance, or activity to feel normal.

6     Denying that the substance, activity, or person is hurting one's life when other people point out the problems.

1     First contact with the substance, person, or activity.

2     Feeling great pleasure with the substance, person, or activity.

8       Feeling miserable or uncomfortable when involved with the substance, person, or activity but not willing to let it or him/ her go.

7       Feeling anxious, depressed, angry, or physically ill when the substance, person, or activity is not available.

9       Friendships, former interest, work, or health suffers because of one's relationship with the person, activity, or substance.

4       Not acknowledging the faults of the substance, person, or activity.

3       Believing that the substance, person, or activity will improve one's life.

## Feeling Word List

| Happy | Sad | Angry | Confused | Scared | Weak | Strong |
|---|---|---|---|---|---|---|
| Alive | Angry | Aggravated | Anxious | Afraid | Ashamed | Active |
| Amused | Apathetic | Annoyed | Awkward | Anxious | Bored | Aggressive |
| Calm | Awful | Burned up | Baffled | Awed | Confused | Alert |
| Cheerful | Bad | Critical | Bothered | Chicken | Defenseless | Angry |
| Content | Blue | Disgusted | Crazy | Confused | Discouraged | Assertive |
| Delighted | Crushed | Enraged | Dazed | Fearful | Embarrassed | Bold |
| Ecstatic | Depressed | Envious | Depressed | Frightened | Exhausted | Brave |
| Excited | Disappointed | Fed up | Disorganized | Horrified | Fragile | Capable |
| Fantastic | Dissatisfied | Frustrated | Disoriented | Insecure | Frail | Confident |
| Fine | Disturbed | Furious | Distracted | Intimidated | Frustrated | Determined |
| Fortunate | Down | Impatient | Disturbed | Jumpy | Guilty | Energetic |
| Friendly | Embarrassed | Irritated | Embarrassed | Lonely | Helpless | Happy |
| Glad | Gloomy | Mad | Frustrated | Nervous | Horrible | Hate |
| Good | Glum | Mean | Helpless | Panicky | Ill | Healthy |
| Great | Hate | Outraged | Lost | Panicked | Impotent | Intense |
| Hopeful | Hopeless | Rage | Mixed up | Shaky | Inadequate | Loud |
| Loving | Hurt | Resentful | Panicky | Shy | Insecure | Love |
| Motherly | Lonely | Sore | Panicked | Stunned | Lifeless | Mean |
| Optimistic | Lost | | Paralyzed | Tense | Lost | Open |
| Peaceful | Low | | Puzzled | Terrified | Overwhelmed | Positive |
| Pleased | Miserable | | Stuck | Threatened | Powerless | Potent |
| Proud | Painful | | Surprised | Timid | Quiet | Powerful |
| Relaxed | Sorry | | Trapped | Uneasy | Run-down | Quick |
| Relieved | Terrible | | Troubled | Unsure | Shaky | Rage |
| Satisfied | Turned off | | Uncertain | Worried | Shy | Secure |
| Thankful | Uneasy | | Uncomfor-table | | Sick | Solid |
| Thrilled | Unhappy | | Unsure | | Timid | Super |
| Turned on | Unloved | | Upset | | Tired | Tough |
| Up | Upset | | Weak | | Unsure | |
| Warm | | | | | Useless | |
| Wonderful | | | | | Vulnerable | |
| | | | | | Wishy-washy | |

# About the Author, John Nielsen

Communication Empowerment
Founder and Director
*www.communication-empowerment.com*

Author of
*Assertive Communications Skills*
and
*Advanced Team-Building / Facilitator
Training Skills*

## John's Qualifications

Success Style Profile—Certified Trainer
see John's Web site at *www.communication-empowerment.com*

Coachville Schools of Coaching—Charter Member
see their Web site at *www.coachville.com*

PREP (Prevention and Relationship Enhancement Program)—Certified Trainer
see their Web site at www.prepinc.com

Prepare/Enrich—Certified Trainer
see their Web site at *www.lifeinnovations.com*

Couple Communication Program—Certified Trainer
see their Web site at *www.couplecommunication.com*

Ordained Minister at Community of Grace Church
see their Web site at *www.icgrace.org*

Business Builder and Team Manager

Leadership Hayward Alumnus (1990), City of Hayward, California

California Southern Baptist Convention—Four years
Executive Board Member

## Life Experiences

From age seventeen until 1986, John struggled with alcohol and drug addiction. From being a successful businessman with a wife and two children, he ended up divorced, bankrupt, and depressed. In 1987, John rededicated his life to Jesus Christ and started on his own recovery journey. In 1989, he began leading programs to help others with relationship and/or addiction issues. John met his current wife Debbie at Community of Grace Church, and they have been happily married since 1993.

John started the healing and recovery ministries at Community of Grace in 1991. Personal and relationship healing have become such a central part of church life that the church went by the nickname "Restoration Depot."

## Business History

As a former marine and business owner, John has a history of successfully leading teams of people to achieve business and organizational goals.

## Largest Regional Distributorship, Western United States

John started as a Safeguard Business Systems distributor in 1970, visiting Northern California businesses, and making presentations to CPA firms to sell manual and computerized accounting systems. As sales increased, he gathered and trained a fifteen-person sales force. By the time he sold the distributorship fourteen years later, it had eleven thousand loyal customers and was the number one Safeguard distributorship in the Western United States.

## Program Facilitator

Based on his proven people skills, the University of Arizona hired John and trained him to conduct drug and alcohol prevention programs for the US Navy and Marines (NADSAP). John conducted forty-hour alcohol and drug prevention workshops for military personnel on bases throughout the Western United States.

## Community-based Recovery Programs

While working for the military drug prevention program, John also facilitated community recovery groups. This eventually became the Steps of Grace Christ-centered twelve-step program at Community of Grace. Steps of Grace currently has twenty-five trained group facilitators leading small support groups for issues ranging from codependency, substance, and sexual addictions to groups for the spouses of addicts and grief recovery. Other recipients of facilitator training have gone on to start recovery groups and programs in their own organizations.

As associate pastor at Community of Grace, John has counseled or coached thousands of people as well as conducting numerous workshops in communication skills and group dynamics. He also trains and mentors other people and organizations in how to lead, coach, counsel, and teach these communication skills workshops.

Visit us at *www.communication-empowerment.com.*

E-mail John Nielsen at *john@communication-empowerment.com.*

## For Future Growth Opportunities Please Go To:

*www.communication-empowerment.com*

### Claim Your Free Video

### And Discover How To Find Out More About The Programs Listed Below

# Programs

### Communication Skills

60 hours of process driven training's designed to help you develop and enhance your communication skills.

### Personal Development

The use of multiple self assessment tools and life coaching allows us to guide you to successful outcomes.

### Team Dynamics

Whether it be team building or conflict resolution learn and develop proven processes for bringing teams together with purpose.

### Train the Trainer

We have a variety of processes and strategies available to purposely train your leaders to get the most out of your teams.

### Healthy Relationships

Whether it be premarital, couples counseling/coaching or mediation, learn how to navigate through complex issues successfully.

### Webinars

Webinar video conferencing focuses on high-end technology for virtual, full-featured meetings that allows the highest level of interaction among participants.

### Mediation

We assist you with your disputes so you can reach mutually acceptable agreements.

# Index

Printed in the United Kingdom
by Lightning Source UK Ltd.
134010UK00001B/124/P

9 781436 3046